Steady Work

by

Karen Gaudet

with

Emily Adams

Published by the Lean Enterprise Institute, Inc.

Lean Enterprise Institute

Book design: Thomas Skehan; Cover design: Mark Karis
Library of Congress Control Number: 2019947451
ISBN: 978-1-934109-60-1

Lean Enterprise Institute, Inc.
27–43 Wormwood Street
Tower Point, Suite 401, Boston, MA 02210
617-871-2900 • fax: 617-871-2999 • lean.org

To Brian, Louis, Hunter, Ethan and Tait ...
I Love you! Mom

CONTENTS

INTRODUCTION

We each face, goodness knows, challenges every day. Some of them are life changing. Some are even life threatening. Most of the challenges we face every day, though, are mundane little things. Get to work. Do our job. Don't mess up. Maybe do something awesome. Hopefully do it better today than yesterday. Get home and deal with whatever drama and joy await us there.

For most of us it doesn't happen often, but, occasionally, overwhelmingly, challenges collide and magnify. They explode. That's what happened to Karen Gaudet and her colleagues at the Starbucks store in the small New England community of Newtown, Connecticut, on December 14, 2012.

Karen had been a devoted Starbucks regional director since 2002. She loved the company, her team, her customers—she loved her job. She had come to love her job even more in the months leading up to the tragic Sandy Hook Elementary School shooting in Newtown on that December day, as she and her team had learned a set of work and management practices that Starbucks called "Playbook." With Playbook, Karen and the teams at the more than 100 stores she managed were learning to serve customers better, more fluidly, with less sweat, fewer mistakes, less drama, all while having more fun and being more deeply engaged in their work.

With over 87,000 different combinations of espresso beverages that a customer may order, being a barista in a Starbucks store was never easy, physically or mentally. But the way employees were originally trained made it more difficult than it needed to be. When Playbook came along, Karen quickly saw it as a means of elevating the work from just getting by to joyfully providing better service for every customer. Even with the ebbs and flows of customer demand shifting throughout each day, Karen and her teams learned how to work steadily through it all. Little did Karen know that steady work would make it possible for her and her team to survive the worst week at work any of them would ever have.

Karen will tell you all about that. And she'll share some practical details about how Playbook made steady work possible for her and her team. But let's back up a bit. How did this Playbook come about? What was Starbucks trying to achieve and why?

Many of Starbucks' successes and a few of its failures are widely known. But just as each store has a back room, each success or failure has a backstory. In 2009, Starbucks was in the middle of a transformative crisis, experiencing severe declining same-store sales in the face of the Great Recession. One of us, Scott, was vice president of global strategy for the executive team of CEO Howard Schultz at the time. Consulting with John, Scott turned the attention of the company to operation of the stores themselves, where value is ultimately created: one store, one customer, and one cup at a time.

As with many companies, the prevailing inclination was to create a centrally developed set of best practices that could be rolled out fast. Instead, the company embraced a new approach leveraging learnings acquired through experiments in lean thinking and practice in a handful of stores.

Starbucks wanted customers to know they could expect the same outstanding customer experience at any Starbucks store (over 7,000 US stores at the time), but they didn't want stores to be cookie-cutter replicas of each other. Every store should be a reflection of the community it served—in design and operations. That thinking, aligned with the team designing stores, resulted in different equipment and layouts. And there were additional differences at each store in terms of basic business fundamentals such as customer demand patterns, product mix, and even the community environment. These patterns not only varied store to store but also were wildly different throughout the day at a single store.

As a result of all the variation, the executive team was convinced that a single solution mandated top-down from corporate could never achieve the outcome they desired. Additionally, Scott and the team wanted store managers and local leadership to have ownership of their business and delivery of improvements. At the same time, Starbucks was understandably concerned that a simplistic empowerment model—telling people to do as they wanted as long as they hit their numbers—however appealing on the surface, would result in unacceptable variability in customer experiences. How could Starbucks, with so many stores that were so different, solve this conundrum? It was clear that a better work system was needed, but how to establish it while avoiding the traps of a top-down, cookie-cutter approach or a traditional empowerment model?

Through experimentation, the team discovered there were some powerful, learnable problem-solving capabilities that would enable local managers to adapt each store's operating system to its local situation, while also enabling responsibility for ongoing improvement. This required development of capability at all levels to solve problems, based on alignment to a core purpose (higher customer value, lower waste, and improved employee experience) and some basic work and leadership principles (e.g., plan-do-check-adjust, leader as coach, pull-based authority, value of routines, and the value of asking *why*, not *who*).

Armed with this capability, managers could take personal ownership to tailor the work system to his or her unique store environment of layout, customer demand, and unique problems. This was Playbook.

Playbook was a new approach for Starbucks—to work and to staffing, as well as to the manager's role in designing, managing, and improving this complete work system. For more than a decade, Starbucks had used the approach to staffing and work assignments that is standard in the food and retail industries: a blunt, top-down labor model, totally out of the hands of store managers, which provided staffing levels by 15-minute intervals along with some high-level role assignment for each team member. But the experiments in trial stores revealed that it was possible to improve financial measures while directly enhancing each customer's experience (beverage quality, speed of delivery, friendliness of staff). These improvements were enabled by deeply engaging the store teams through building their problem-solving capability.

Playbook provided the basic building blocks for managers to refine and choreograph these elements in what was essentially a big Tetris board for their specific customer demand patterns (drink mix and transaction levels). This not only allowed store managers to create their own work system but also provided a deep understanding of how to schedule staff to meet their unique customer profile. With this deeper understanding of the nuances of work methods and a system to improve it, store managers could improve their financial, customer, and employee performance. Neither top-down mandate nor bottom-up empowerment, the path Starbucks chose was something decidedly in between.

As Karen describes in these pages, Playbook was a truly empowering methodology that was owned by each employee who was touched by it. It wasn't a competitive strategy separate from daily operations tactics—it was an integrated strategy that fostered problem solving at every level of the company. The work and management transformation in Starbucks' stores had several important phases, each designed to introduce additional layers of learning, from teaching some basic practices to a structured process to engage and develop leaders such as Karen.

This book is Karen's story. It's a story that is both deeply emotional and imminently practical. It's the story of one leader's unique experience of learning and then leading others through the same learning experience. And it's the story of a leader helping teams develop steady work to help them get through normal days just a little bit better and help make the worst day ever at work just a little bit bearable. Who wouldn't want steady work like that?

Scott Heydon, Mercer Island, Seattle, Washington
John Shook, Central Square, Cambridge, Massachusetts
September 2019

Learning to See the Perfect Latte

The circle of faces around me leaned in as I lifted the pitcher of cold milk closer to a metal wand pumping out 190-degree steam. The perfect latte requires precisely steamed milk. I said, "See, the tip of the steaming wand needs to skim just below the surface of the milk, making a shushing noise. Just like a piece of paper being ripped in two."

I held my breath and brought the milk closer. The wand skated under the milky surface once, twice, and then my nerves betrayed me. My hand holding the metal pitcher bounced. The wand sunk deep into the milk and hit the interior side of the pitcher, and the milk screamed like a newborn calf.

"OK," I said, trying to grin. "That's how *not* to do it."

One of my district managers, David, smiled encouragingly. But I'm pretty sure that a smirk crossed the face of a store manager in this downtown Hartford, Connecticut, café. Most of the people here had actually been Starbucks baristas. They were more experienced with a steam wand. Who was I to give this training?

On this February evening in 2008, I was a regional director for Starbucks, responsible for about 110 stores in the Northeast. It had been six years since I had (briefly) made lattes in my original training. So, I was rusty. But I was here, leading this retraining, so that we would all be making beverages the right way, I explained. I shook my hand where the steam had burned it and tried again.

We were relearning how to spot a bad shot of espresso, how to avoid screaming milk, because Howard Shultz had just returned as CEO of Starbucks and announced that we needed to get back to our roots. On one day, we shut down operations in about 8,000 stores across the United States for sessions such as this. Some people called it a publicity stunt. But it was the beginning of a profound shift in the way we worked.

It was not clear to me then, but what we were really learning was to see the work together—to create a common understanding about what was right and what was not right. This would eventually lead to solving problems in a new way. I was also learning how to be vulnerable in front of a team, to admit that I did not always know what I was doing and that other people might have better solutions.

Over the next five years, my fellow executives, managers, baristas, and I would learn the basic principles of lean thinking and how to apply Toyota Production System techniques to some of our operations. We created islands of excellence that often wobbled and fell. Then, we implemented a management system to support frontline standardization and witnessed the power of an interdependent operating system—one that was reliant on all of its parts, which stabilized and balanced the work while exposing problems for us to address. Together we created work with a steady cadence built on standardized routines that was able to absorb the busiest hours at Starbucks. Steady work was the true revelation of our experiments, and, on the worst week of our lives, it saved us.

During those years, I discovered the profound and maddeningly elusive power of standardization in a service industry. I saw what is required to keep standardized operations running and how the discipline could change us if we allowed it.

But first, we all had to learn how to pull the perfect shot of espresso that would coat the back of a spoon like honey. After all, this was the work.

* * *

It is easier now, in hindsight, to see what a pivotal moment February of 2008 was for Starbucks. Opened in 1971 in Seattle as a seller of freshly roasted coffee, Starbucks changed owners and morphed into a seller of coffee beverages in 1987. Over the next 20 years, it expanded into the daily lives of millions of people.

Café lattes in paper cups were suddenly everywhere. All over the country, people embraced the coffeehouse culture, setting up their laptops and settling in for hours. Starbucks began talking about its stores as a third place in American life—like a church or a library, a place outside of home and work where communities gathered. They emphasized human connections.

And the company grew. The Frappuccino and the Pumpkin Spice Latte arrived. In the decade of 1998–2008, Starbucks opened an average of four new stores every single day and expanded its market from Japan and Brazil to Saudi Arabia and Russia, all while emphasizing fair-trade coffee and sustainable farming practices. The company went public in 1992, and as the stock price soared, stocks split and split again in the first four years.

In the Northeast, where I managed ten districts of 10–15 stores each, we saw 12%–18% sales growth year over year. In my Brookline, Massachusetts district, which covered the area between Fenway Park and Boston College, sales grew by 15% year over year without adding a single store. In the rest of my districts, we were adding at least one store every month.

My job in those years—from 2002–2008—was consumed with the logistics of opening new stores. I worked with the in-house real estate team and my crew of about 10 district managers to select new sites, hire new partners, and add a dozen or more new stores a year. When a district manager had more than 10 stores, we created a new district and (usually) elevated a store manager to lead it. When I had more than 10 districts, we split off part of my region and promoted a district manager to regional director. We were creating approximately one new district every year. Still, we grew.

Starbucks added dozens of new seasonal flavored beverages, breakfast sandwiches, CDs, and books. Our store managers received a 300-page glossy promotional book every eight weeks that introduced new drinks, new coffee roasts, new music compilations, and movie promotions. We had drive-through stores, mall stores, community coffee houses; we opened licensed stores in airports, grocery stores, and universities.

And then in 2007, along with the rest of the world's economy, Starbucks stumbled. A new store in Connecticut opened to surprisingly laconic sales. We failed to hit revenue targets in a number of locations. Along with the district managers, I went into stores and talked to baristas, asking whether they were doing the usual community outreach, whether they were offering free samples. They were doing everything the same way it had always been done.

Our instinct was to extend store hours, create new outreach initiatives, offer more samples. Nothing seemed to work. Memos from executives at Starbucks headquarters in Seattle warned of ominous signs in the national economy.

By the fall of 2007, when the nation's bankers were being questioned in front of congressional committees on live television, the damage to our economy was already clear to us. As the Great Recession took hold and neighborhoods were suddenly peppered with foreclosed homes, people cut back on their three-cup-a-day habit or gave up the daily luxury of a perfect single-shot vanilla latte. The company that could do nothing but win was suffering a sharp correction.

In coffeehouses around the Northeast, our employees were worried. They saw neighbors losing their homes. Jobs in formerly stable industries were being eliminated. For many people, a part-time job at Starbucks had been a reliable source of healthcare benefits, the little extra needed to fill out a family's income or to help a student through college. For others, it was a full-time career. If their neighbors could not afford a latte, how would we survive?

We responded, in part, by relearning the craft of making a perfect espresso beverage. To do this, Starbucks shut down thousands of stores across the country in February 2008 and asked leaders like me—newly retrained—to lead the training. Journalists responded with a collective gasp. Businesses were supposed to cut costs and headcounts in recessions rather than spend money on developing employees.

To understand how unique Starbucks' reaction to the Great Recession was, you need to know a little about the quick-serve restaurant (QSR) industry. While Starbucks held itself out as anything but fast food, this was the category we belonged to, and it was where I had been working for 20 years before Starbucks.

* * *

Starting out in high school restocking the salad bar at my local Bonanza Steakhouse in central Connecticut, I went on to work my way through the many layers of management at Burger King and Wendy's restaurants and then franchise groups. Working for franchise owners who had 15–25 restaurants, I was accustomed to a hard-numbers, no-nonsense approach to management. In QSR, labor costs were considered fat that should be trimmed as tight as possible.

In fact, all costs were considered bad. Once, when I was on vacation, a franchise owner—let's call him Mr. Brown—called me, furious. He had been in one of his New Hampshire stores and noticed that there were paper cups in the kitchen trash cans, indicating that employees had been consuming beverages on the job.

Now, this particular store was high performing. It made a lot of money for Mr. Brown. On weekday afternoons it was mostly staffed by local moms who were making extra money while their kids were in school. These women were good workers, organized and thoughtful. Sometimes, they were thirsty. When Mr. Brown visited and saw those paper cups in the trash, he proceeded to dump out all the trash cans in the kitchen and count the cups. He made a big scene. Then he called me with an extrapolated cost of those cups over a year and shouted something like, "There's $100 in there. What do you propose to do about that?"

I proposed to find another job; this time as director of operations for a start-up that mined point-of-sale (POS) data from QSR cash registers and made useful software. That's where my education in the quick-serve sector really expanded. I was working with big-name fast-food chains all over the East Coast and Midwest, talking with everyone from executives to frontline employees to understand their work in detail, then training them on software and testing results.

For these restaurants, high turnover was a fact of life. Kitchens can be dirty and dangerous places to work. Store managers were often absent; positions went unfilled, or managers ran two stores at once, mostly because their jobs were high pressure and did not pay well enough for the amount of daily firefighting that was required. Without good oversight, I saw food handlers pouring hot grease into paper receptacles—filtering the oil to clean and reuse it—and working in conditions that gave me indigestion.

This was not the overt disrespect of Mr. Brown—turning over trash cans in the kitchen or throwing a head of lettuce across the room to make a point. But poor training and disorganized, highly pressured work environments are just as disrespectful as shouting.

Maybe it is human nature for owners to focus obsessively on shrinking the biggest numbers on their accounts-payable sheets, such as labor. But in the fast-food industry there is a tendency to forget that these are people on the front line—people with families and dreams and needs.

Managers were sometimes told to focus on employee retention and offered bonuses if their stores stayed fully staffed. But they were given no direction on *how* to do this. They were just told to stop losing people. At the same time, owners were implementing new labor-scheduling software that kept people working shorter, more frequent, and unpredictable shifts.

New schedules came out every week. People were asked to work three hours one night and then four hours the next morning, closing the restaurant at 11 p.m. only to return at 4 a.m. for their next shift, without thought to their transportation, sleep needs, or childcare challenges. In this sector, employees were units of labor, not people. I knew there had to be a better way; I just had not seen it yet.

Then I found Starbucks, which had turned that model on its head. The coffee chain that I joined in 2002 was in the business to make money, of course. But not at the expense of people. As a regional director, a big part of my job was to make sure that people who worked for us were respected.

At Starbucks, everyone who worked at least 20 hours a week was offered healthcare benefits and help with college tuition. We received bonuses and stock options that made all of us partners in the company. That's how we referred to Starbucks employees: *partners*. We were expected to know the personal concerns of our partners. Managers were judged on the strength and depth of our relationships with our direct reports. Forcing a partner to work a last-minute shift under threat of job loss was unthinkable.

With a commitment to opening every new Starbucks store with 70% experienced baristas, we needed to move people around a lot. A new store in southern Massachusetts, for instance, might open with baristas commuting short-term from Rhode Island and Connecticut. Around 70% of partners hired for the new store, meanwhile, worked through their training periods at more established stores nearby. When we opened a more remote store, in the Berkshires of Western Massachusetts or in Vermont, we put together a "star team" of baristas and put them up in a local hotel while they worked and trained new partners.

We were always hiring, developing, training, and promoting people in those early years. My goal was to have a talent bench that was two-deep on all levels. That meant I was mentoring two possible replacements for myself and that all of my district managers had identified two store managers that they were coaching toward becoming a district manager. Store managers were training their two shift supervisors to lead a store, and the best baristas were being trained as supervisors.

Our focus on people was external, as well. We made community connections to market the brand. We brought coffee and snacks to walk-a-thons, festivals, school functions, and service groups. If partners believed in a nonprofit organization enough to donate a lot of hours, the company donated money. In those days before Starbucks began advertising, in fact, this was our growth strategy: being active, visible community members.

Every good company knows that it is selling more than just a product. Companies sell assurances of quality, ideas about lifestyle, and a sense of belonging. At Starbucks, we focused on connecting with people. We developed relationships with regular customers. Baristas were not judged solely on their ability to make a Venti extra-dry cappuccino. Greeting repeat customers by name, and remembering favorite beverages and families were part of the job because our real business was people.

Howard Behar, a former president of Starbucks, used to say that we were not a coffee business serving people; we were a people business serving coffee. It was a philosophy that made a very large chain of QSRs seem like neighborhood businesses, and it made Starbucks wildly successful.

The respect for employees, community outreach, and all that delicious coffee added up to a kind of happiness that I did not know was possible at work. I spent my first few years at Starbucks waiting for the other shoe to drop. Was it possible for people to actually be this genuine and nice at work—to adopt kindness as a corporate policy? I loved my job. I wanted to protect the company and its mission. Therefore, it was impossible for me to ignore our problems.

In the years of rapid growth, too many stores had long lines of people waiting at the register or milling around in front of the espresso bar during the morning rush. Sometimes lines of people stretched outside the doors. Long waits meant unhappy customers. Brewed coffee sometimes sat for too long, even though our policy was to have coffee brewed fresh every 30 minutes. Coffee that sits even 10 minutes past its prime can taste burned or bitter. All the pastries and hip soundtracks in the world cannot cover for bad coffee.

Still, Starbucks grew and churned some incredible profits. Until, suddenly, it did not.

* * *

As the Great Recession kept worsening in 2008, we closed 10 stores in my Northeast region alone. This was a few months after the latte retraining. Partners in closing stores were all offered jobs in nearby locations, but some chose a severance package rather than move to a different location. A district manager and several support-staff members were laid off. Nobody was escorted immediately to the door. They were given time and space to process what was happening and say goodbye, plus assistance finding new employment.

Ten years after the fact, I can report these events as a series of abstract numbers and facts. But at the time, every day felt awful, and my confidence in the company I had grown to love was diminished. Decisions about where and how to cut were agonizing. I wondered, was this the proverbial other shoe dropping?

It was. But it turns out that the shoe did not look at all like I thought it would. In another restaurant chain, the dropping shoe would have been a boot. Benefits and hours would be cut. Higher-wage, experienced employees would be laid off. Training for new employees would be reduced, and, inevitably, the restaurants would become less organized, dirtier, and more frantic. I have seen restaurant chains react badly to small downturns in the stock market, to say nothing of the Great Recession.

Starbucks, however, began introducing us to lean thinking. In the fall of 2007, I was sent a PowerPoint presentation about the work of scooping ice cream—where value was added, where waste occurred. It was a little mysterious in that I was not sure what I was supposed to do with it.

Then in February of 2008, as we conducted retraining for all employees, it became clear that Starbucks' senior management was seriously thinking about how work was actually being done.

Consider the milk. Steamed milk is the heart of most coffee beverages. Espresso may be the soul, but people fall in love with specific attributes of steamed milk. The cappuccino drinker wants just a kiss of warm milk and a cloud of foam to slowly melt into the drink. The latte drinker wants more milk and a creamy dollop of foam on top. And everyone wants their skim or whole milk, almond milk or soy, to be just the right temperature to bring out the inherent sweetness. Steaming milk is the trickiest and most time-consuming task of making an espresso beverage.

Therefore, it made sense to many baristas, as we discovered, to steam a large pitcher full of whole milk, using a portion for the current drink and setting aside the rest for another order. If the next six orders were for drinks with skim milk, soy, or no milk at all, that pitcher would sit cooling on the counter.

If the milk was repeatedly re-steamed, it could taste a little like tin. If the barista dipped the wand too far into the milk and made that screaming noise, the milk would burn—even just a little—and lose much of its sweetness. If the milk was not re-steamed and a drink was a few degrees cooler than our best practice, the customer might not send it back, but they would not be happy either.

Steaming too much milk at once was not the right way, but some of the baristas who did it this way were like rock stars—able to muscle through a rush while chatting with repeat customers and remembering everyone's favorite drink. When star baristas showed new partners how they worked, their methods were copied. And that is how stores and then maybe a whole district fell away from the proper method of steaming just enough milk for one or two beverages, tops.

People who are accustomed to lean thinking will recognize this as backsliding from one-piece flow to batch processing. We know from long experience that making elements of the finished product, such as steamed milk, in batches might seem efficient, but it creates a lot of waste. Especially when it comes to making fresh food and drink, batch processing is a sure path to stale waste. (Just think of premade burgers sitting under a hot lamp.)

We—the directors and district managers—needed to get close to the work to see important details, such as the fact that some baristas were using large metal pitchers for steaming milk instead of smaller two-drink-at-a-time pitchers. By getting so close to the work that we could teach it, we had conversations about how and why bad practices were adopted, giving us insight to the root cause of problems for baristas and customers.

At the end of 2008, we learned how to observe partners making brewed coffee and discovered a mountain of wasted coffee just in the bean-grinding practices. Then we examined all the work elements that went into making brewed coffee every 30 minutes and set about doing it better. Next, we examined how the pastry case was restocked. We were learning to apply lean thinking to individual processes, and it made sense, to a point.

By the end of 2009, we had examined the work of espresso drinks, brewed coffee, and restocking pastries and improved those processes. We were learning more about how to look at work and build good work sequences, but the improved work stood alone as islands of excellence. Unsupported by the rest of our habits, the improved processes were difficult to maintain.

Then in 2010 we began implementing a lean operating system called "Playbook" that was based on the Toyota Production System. This would knit our islands of excellence together with a new management system and daily problem solving. (I'll explain this in chapter 3.) From the beginning, I was a true believer. But that does not mean it was a perfect system.

In fact, the experience of implementing an integrated lean system in more than 100 stores across New England—and then coaching its implementation in another 500—raised some very interesting questions about standardized work and human beings in the service industry that leaders need to explore. In all industries, getting people to perform tasks in the same sequence and at the same rate every time—i.e., standard work—has been problematic. Humans just are not hardwired for repetition, it seems. And in service industries, quality human contact is central to the work. Human contact and standardization can seem like oil and water.

But here is the truly important discovery from our observations: when task standardization is adopted and steady work cadences are achieved, people are freer to do the satisfying work of making human connections. When work tasks are both repeatable and rote, managers, executives, and frontline baristas all have more space in their lives to chat a little, to ask questions, and to listen to others.

This became most evident to me during the worst week of our lives. When Newtown, Connecticut, became the epicenter of a horrific tragedy in December 2012, people needed our store to meet and mourn. This happens a lot to coffeehouses; they have become a town's public house. In this case, we went from serving something like 500 espresso beverages a day to 1,500.

In chapter 5, I will explain exactly how we accommodated the increased demand. But here, I should say that we did not change our menu offerings. We still made those labor-intensive, comforting lattes. We did increase the number of partners working but did not simply throw extra people into the mix. By this time, we understood the work well enough that we could divide tasks between the different roles—barista, cashier, store support, etc.—and change the mix quickly when needed.

Using techniques from the Playbook, we were able to ramp up operations and serve everyone who came into the store—from grieving families and townspeople to the international press—as well as carting out to-go urns of coffee to first responders and to memorials and other gatherings. With the help of standardization, we were able to provide the best comfort we could.

In similar situations, our stores have become overwhelmed. A café near the finish line of the 2013 Boston Marathon, which looked out on a scene of dozens of injuries from a terrorist bombing attack just a few months after the Newtown mass shooting, struggled to handle increased traffic. That store was shut down by the City of Boston for several days as part of the crime scene. It reopened to greater demand. Staff members were not yet trained in the way of the Playbook, however. Without the comfort of standardized work routines, and without the deeper understanding of how to respond to sudden swells in demand, our partners struggled with the work even as they were dealing with a lot of raw emotions.

While introducing the lean operating system in stores across New England, we saw people embrace this style of working wholeheartedly and others chafe at it. I learned a lot about how standardization succeeds and fails. I studied deploying best practices versus teaching best thinking and learned to train managers to think rather than automate management decisions through software. And I discovered some important things about happiness and work, too.

The first and most important thing for managers and partners is to understand the work itself—the precise tasks involved in creating value for customers.

Throwing Out Coffee

In the fall of 2008, with the economy in tatters and a lot of us still feeling battered by layoffs and store closings, my colleagues and I arrived at a very large, elaborately staged company gathering. This was not the first time Starbucks had hosted a leadership conference that called together all store managers, district managers, regional directors, and top executives—nearly 10,000 people—into a single place for a week. But the timing was unsettling.

Added to our internal anxieties was the location. As the biggest coffee port in the country, New Orleans was a great city for us. But it was still devastated from Hurricane Katrina three years earlier. Yards were filled with storm debris; many houses were still boarded up, waiting for builders and funds. How they found hotel rooms for all of us in that struggling city I do not know.

Even before we arrived, there was a lot of criticism of Starbucks—a publicly held company—for spending money at a time like this. Sales were down and we had overbuilt, creating too many new stores. And yet, when we arrived in New Orleans, there were welcoming gift bags for each of the 8,000 store managers, 900 district managers, and 120 regional directors like me.

At the convention center, there were four huge interactive galleries, decorated with enormous banners and colorful photos, and with displays telling the story of coffee. There was an enormous coffee roaster, hundreds of coffee trees planted in huge containers, and a mocked-up bean-drying area where we could rake through pounds of raw coffee beans just like they do in Indonesia or

Rwanda. It was hard to look at the trappings and not think of all the people who had been laid off a few months earlier.

And yet, Starbucks is a company filled with enthusiastic people. Waves of excitement were almost visible in the main hall as we all gathered together. One after another, top executives took the stage and told us we were on the cusp of a new era—not another time of runaway growth but of doubling down on our core values. Howard Shultz admitted that we had strayed from our founding principles and that not all of our problems of the past year were due to the economy. We would return to people, community, and good coffee.

All good, but how were we going to do that?

Cliff Burrows, president of Starbucks' US business, gave us the first clue. He said that we had a great opportunity to learn more about how our partners were doing the work of brewing coffee. We would learn how to observe and simplify processes. From there we would not just make better coffee, we would make better work for our partners.

In breakout sessions with fellow regional directors and district managers, I was introduced to spaghetti mapping to trace the path of people as they did their jobs. We learned about waste in the work process and how movement did not necessarily add value for the customer. We learned what to count and how to measure wasted coffee and dairy products.

This might seem like a tedious task to some. But to me, it was a welcome shift in focus. Instead of piling on more specialty drinks or new stores, we were getting tools to focus on the work and help our often-overworked baristas. Whether these tools would ultimately help us get control of the chaos I did not know. But at least we were moving in a positive direction.

Then, we went out together in teams and helped clean yards and parks and neighborhoods around New Orleans. Every day, 2,000 of us were rotated through work crews. I remember clearing thick brambles out of a front yard while all around me, my colleagues were scraping, painting, and helping to unearth a beautiful city. It was hard, sweaty work, and it filled me with joy.

For the final general session of the conference, the musician and activist Bono came on stage and spoke of a new business model that united commerce and compassion. Starbucks was a company that was holding onto its values even while seeking profits, Bono said. A for-profit company working within a capitalist system really could make the world a better place, he said. I am quite sure that everyone heard and believed that message, and we carried it with us as we flew home.

* * *

Our local transformation began, of course, with a coffee tasting. Within a week of the conference, I gathered my 10 district managers around a press pot of Anniversary Blend. A lush, full-bodied blend of beans from Indonesia and Papua New Guinea with a spicy kick of aged Sumatra, the coffee paired well with many foods, and we each brought a dish to sample. Money was still tight, so it was a potluck lunch. But that did not matter. We were all still high on the energy and emotion of New Orleans as we put together a game plan to go see the work of brewing coffee.

Unlike past new programs at Starbucks, which were introduced to store managers with all the personal touch of an email or a glossy mass-mailed publication, this one was to be leader-led. And it had to be quick. Every store manager had to learn to observe work, take measurements, and report back quickly.

Each district manager selected a "seed store" where I would join them for a day of observation. Together, we arrived in the predawn darkness to see the day's setup. Using pads of paper to trace the steps of the store manager and a barista onto a spaghetti map, we watched a process that seemed logical enough.

It began with the beans. Every day there were two types of coffee on offer: a decaf and a bold roast. The latter could be any one of a half-dozen types of coffee from around the world, usually selected by the store manager. For the 14 hours that the store would be open, these two coffees needed to be made fresh every 30 minutes.[1] A good setup was crucial.

Out from the storeroom would come a silver five-pound bag of coffee beans that we called a bullet. Based on experience and intuition, the store manager would decide how much brewed coffee might be consumed that day and start grinding that amount. In the Northeast, people drank a lot of brewed coffee, and nobody wanted to hold up an afternoon rush by stopping to grind more beans for brewing, so a partner usually spent about 30 minutes grinding the entire bullet.

It was a wonderful smell: all that fresh coffee being ground before it was packed into cube-shaped plastic containers and tightly sealed. The cubes were then stacked on the counter for easy access.

Just before opening the doors, a partner would brew two batches of coffee. For each, they would set a timer for 30 minutes, scoop ground coffee into the paper filter, put it in the basket, slide the basket into the machine, select the batch size on the machine, position the urn underneath, and press *go*.

---

1. A few years earlier, company policy was that coffee should be made fresh every hour. An executive in Seattle changed that policy to 30-minute cycles. Store managers were told to carry out the policy without guidance on how to make it happen, on top of their existing work.

According to our stopwatches, it took about one minute to prepare the coffee maker and seven minutes for the coffee to brew. When it was finished, there would be 22 minutes before that timer went off. Whoever was free would then dump out any remaining coffee, set the timer, scoop coffee, load the machine, press go, and then do the same for the decaf. (If a guest ordered a brewed decaf during the seven-minute machine cycle, we would say, "It's brewing." Guests had a lot more patience with that answer, we found, than being told that coffee was unavailable.)

To measure waste, we gave each store two clear plastic two-gallon pitchers to pour excess coffee into before partners started a new batch. So, a partner would hear the timer, dump coffee, set the timer, scoop coffee, put the basket into the machine, and press go.

This pattern would hold for maybe one or two cycles before the contradictions set in. Remember that our message to all partners was that the customers' needs came before all else. Personal connection was our specialty.

So, what were baristas supposed to do when a timer went off while they were facing a line of four beverage orders and the cashier had a line five people deep? Maybe in this instance, three people are on shift. If that third person was cleaning the bathroom, or doing dishes in back, or any one of a dozen other necessary tasks, there is a good chance that someone would reset the timer for a minute just to make the beeping stop. And the coffee would sit.

In every store I went to, I watched the same dynamic. The timers were constantly interrupting. It was like hearing my teenage son's morning alarm go off down the hall over and over again as he kept hitting snooze, and I wanted to yell, "Get up, already!" What's worse than a ringing alarm?

Partners were caught in a pinch. Should they ignore the customer in front of them in order to brew a fresh batch? Should they serve slightly stale coffee or make a guest wait while a fresh pot is brewed? Many partners were in the habit of offering an Americano[2] instead but ringing it up as brewed coffee. It made some guests happy but made inventory and sales inaccurate.

There was another complication. We were encouraged to send out big to-go urns of coffee—called travelers—to community events. In many stores, we also had frequent to-go orders for coffee and pastries for office meetings. When we needed to make extra brewed coffee, the half-hour cadence for brewing was thrown off.

All day long, our partners were running back and forth, accompanied by the inevitable ringing of the timers, making dozens of decisions about who should make coffee and when, and wondering, how old was the decaf in the pot, anyway? At the end of the day, they would dump the brewed coffee, wash the urns, and then throw out any remaining coffee that had been ground that morning. They also tossed out all the dairy products that had been sitting on the counter. The waste was staggering.

It was common for partners to throw out between one and two pounds of ground coffee at the end of the day. Another half-gallon of dairy products would often get tossed at the end of every shift. That was a gallon of dairy product, along with a pound or two of coffee, wasted every day, every store, across my region of 110 stores.

Measuring the waste—seeing the numbers add up on our spreadsheets—was galvanizing. The executive in charge of North American operations had committed to reducing waste in US stores by $25 million. We were learning that there was a lot of opportunity.

2. An Americano is a shot of espresso—or two or three, depending on size of the cup—with hot water filling the rest of the cup.

After every one of my district managers had seen the work with me, they visited each of their stores and taught the same observation techniques to their store managers, who, in turn, enlisted the help of all partners to measure wasted motion, coffee, and dairy, as well as stock-outs.[3] Every time partners had to say we did not have fresh decaf or bold roast, they put a hash mark on a piece of paper. Except it did not always happen.

This transfer of observation studies to the store partners was not accomplished perfectly. People who had been to New Orleans had a vision of what we were trying to accomplish and could see the work in context. But I have to admit, we did not always communicate it very well to frontline partners. As we collected data on the time and motion involved in doing the work, partners saw stopwatches and felt eyes on them while working. They waited for judgment, which never feels good. During those weeks, the district managers and I visited several stores where partners were anxious, and we tried to explain the studies and what we hoped to accomplish. We soothed their fears as best we could.

It did not take long, thankfully, before partners were improving the process of measuring. Instead of papers and hash tags, people installed plastic cups next to cash registers, and partners put a coffee bean in the cup every time they had to say, "No," or "I'm sorry but we're out of that." The bean method usually worked.

In store after store, managers began this exercise assuming that at day's end there would be 10 beans in the cup at the very most. I knew the problems we were having with reliable deliveries, though, and was ready to hear that up to 10% of day's orders began with telling a customer, "Sorry."

---

3. "Stock-out" is a common term in retail, meaning that a customer desires an item that is suddenly not in stock. In a grocery store, this would be an empty spot on the shelf. In coffee stores, it means that there is no fresh-brewed coffee to sell.

When my district managers reported back on observations from all 100+ stores, however, we were all stunned to see that the number of customers who could not get what they originally wanted was more like 25%–30%. Meanwhile, gallons of brewed coffee were being poured down the drain at every store. It felt like we spent the day throwing out coffee and telling people we did not have any.

* * *

The next step began, of course, with a coffee tasting. From our home offices, seven of my fellow regional directors and I poured ourselves cups of Gold Coast blend from our press pots and slurped it loudly over a conference call. It's a bold blend of coffees from Indonesia and Latin America with a little sweetness of dark Italian roast. And then we talked over the results from stores across the Northeast. The sum-up was that nearly 1,000 stores were following the same routines in the Northeast: grind beans in the morning, set timers, make coffee.

All of us had seen partners working all day to a constant backdrop of timers ringing, pouring coffee down the drain, and then being forced to say, "Can you wait for us to make a fresh batch? No? How about an Americano?" We had spreadsheets drenched in wasted coffee. Nobody on the call felt great about the predicament our frontline partners faced dozens of times a day.

During this time, all regional directors were also attending more advanced lean training. We were learning about tools and theories, reading John Shook's book *Managing to Learn*, and working our way through A3s to solve complex problems. It was unnerving at first. My peers and I had all advanced to this stage in our careers by having good solutions. Now, we were supposed to simply expose our problems to each other and be comfortable with the problem-solving process. This was a lot more challenging than simply having the "right" answer.

Then, while still unsure how useful these A3s would be, I turned around to teach them to my team of district managers. We used those A3s to begin attacking some of the problems. We moved coffee grinders closer to the brewing machines, and many stores stopped pre-grinding a whole bullet before the store opened. It helped. But the overall issue—providing fresh coffee every 30 minutes without fail and without wasting beans and while giving our partners a better work experience—was daunting.

Still without a single solution, we were asked to report our findings to the team in Seattle. And maybe that was the right call, since most of us did not know enough about lean thinking to take the next step. But it was disconcerting. After two decades spent coming up with good answers, my job was now to find errors and waste in my stores and simply report it to my bosses. This felt dangerous to my career. How would they reply?

* * *

In April 2009, the answer was sent from Seattle as a PowerPoint presentation. Called "A Better Way," the slides detailed the new method for keeping freshly brewed coffee available at all times. And since this was Starbucks, where adding new products was an article of faith, the better way came with a new standard coffee to be added to the mix.

Pike's Place blend had actually been introduced amid great fanfare several months earlier. A pop-up Starbucks store had been erected in New York City's Bryant Square Park, and free samples were handed out by the thousands. This was to be a cornerstone of brewed-coffee consistency in our stores. Instead of facing a choice of one of a half-dozen bold-roast coffees, guests could count on seeing Pike's Place on the menu, as well as decaf and bold. This meant we would now have three pots of coffee that had to be fresh at all times.

The first waste-reduction technique was for all stores to grind beans fresh for every pot. No more mornings spent grinding an entire bullet and then dumping out pounds of ground coffee at the end of the day. This was also a quality improvement. Taste tests showed that people could tell the difference between coffee samples made with fresh-ground beans and beans that had been ground eight hours earlier. And this way, stores would be filled with the scent of freshly ground beans all day.

These were good changes, but I was acutely aware that we were adding more work for our partners. How could we achieve both speed and consistency during the brewing process?

The way to do this, according to A Better Way, was by setting a cadence. If there were three types of coffee to make, and each took eight minutes to set up and brew, and every urn had to be remade after 24 minutes, then a partner had to prepare brewed coffee every eight minutes throughout the day. Knowing this forced us to throw out our old ad hoc methods and assign the task of brewing coffee to an individual on every shift.

To avoid waste, we also needed to pre-figure batch sizes. Store managers used POS data to look at how much brewed coffee was sold during each half-hour time frame during weekdays and on weekends. This could vary widely from store to store. Then, the store managers could forecast how much decaf, bold, and Pike's Place needed to be made throughout the day, create a chart, and hang it at the brewing station for partners to reference.

This was pretty straightforward, but the question remained about who should brew. Let's say there are three people on shift in a store: a barista making espresso drinks, a cashier taking orders, and a floater.[4] In the past, the floater's main responsibility was to support the cashier and barista. They also kept the café and bathroom clean, cleared and washed dishes, restocked the pastry case and cold case with drinks and food, etc. Now the floater's job might be to prepare coffee every eight minutes and do the other tasks in between.

It was just as easy and as difficult as that. We had all done the observation studies. We drew snarled spaghetti charts and knew the amount of waste we were generating. Doing those observations helped to remove much of the emotion that is often present in telling people exactly how to do their jobs. That meant teams in the stores could look at the situation as a common problem and decide, for instance, to reassign certain tasks to the cashier or barista instead of the floater. If the floater cleaned the bathroom during a slow cycle, the barista could make two rounds of fresh-brewed coffee, giving their partner 16 minutes to clean.

In many ways, A Better Way provided clarity about the work. If the brewing partner needed 10 or 20 minutes for a task or a break, we all knew that someone else had to make the coffee for one or two cycles. The brewing partner could simply ask a coworker, "Will you take the next three timers while I clean up?"

But what happens when there are just two people on shift, as is often the case in smaller stores? Or, during the rush at a busy drive-through, there were often two-hour stretches when losing the assistance of one person for one minute every seven minutes created

---

4. This is a person assigned to do whatever needs to be done in the moment, from cleaning the store to restocking and assisting behind the counter.

longer lines? A lot of drive-through QSRs would add staff for those two hours. But Starbucks was not inclined to strong-arm people into two-hour shifts.

In short, this Better Way had come with precise instructions as to how to do the work of brewed coffee, but it quickly became clear that we still did not know how to support that work.

And so we entered a time that I came to think of as the Blizzard of Best Practices. Starbucks employed a lot of very smart, generous people. And there were thousands of us all across the country who were confronting similar problems. We shared our solutions with regional leaders or the team in Seattle, and they broadcast the best solutions back to the stores.

For instance, a store manager in Indiana might have decided that the best place for the brewed-coffee timer was at the cash register. We would all be invited to follow suit. (Even if it meant that cashiers were often resetting timers without telling the brewer to make a new pot.) Another store decided that the cashier, who was closest to the brewing station, should be the brewer. Or, at drive-up stores with three people working the window, coffee brewing should be assigned to the support position furthest from the customer. Also, to sell more whole-bean coffee, we should place three one-pound bags of coffee in easy reach at each register. In order to ensure that we were giving out enough free samples, we should start every day with 100 sample cups stacked on the back counter, to create a visual cue for baristas to make samples.

The good ideas kept coming at us. There were too many to fully digest, much less implement. And some of those good ideas bore no relation to the problems of 100 stores. Store managers naturally chose some best practices and ignored others. So, an initiative that was intended to create a consistent experience for the customer was actually creating slightly different operations in every store. That might be all right if the end result was the same. But for our partners, who often filled in at nearby stores when needed, those best practices created new operations to relearn in each location.

Brewed coffee was not the only work routine subjected to A Better Way. In Seattle, the headquarters lean team—Josh Howell, Hollie Jenson, Brent Moden, and Scott Heydon, who jointly designed Starbucks' lean operating system and its initial rollout—dedicated time to reviewing and revising the way that the pastry case was loaded. They created a better work sequence and sent it out to all the stores.

A Better Way to make espresso beverages was a bigger change. Baristas were used to adding their own flair, but in general, partners would grab a cup, pump syrup, add espresso shots, and add the steamed milk. Now, milk was to be steamed in a specific routine: pour milk to the first line, steam with shushing sound for five seconds, then pull pitcher down, wipe the steam wand, press a button to send a cleansing burst of steam through wand, then pull the espresso shot. Next, cue up the espresso shots, and while the machine works, add syrup to the cup. As the espresso was dropping out of the machine, steam milk for next beverage. Then grab cup one, add espresso and then steamed milk, and call out the customer's name.

So, the work order of building a beverage did not change. Baristas still added syrup, coffee, and a dairy product to the cup in that order. Now, however, they were using the machine's cycle time to begin work on the next beverage before the first one was complete. For some baristas, the repeated routine helped them make beverages more consistently. Others chafed at the strictures.

The Better Ways were all improvements to some extent, but most of us were still unclear on how to support the work. We were always missing some important element in the work sequence. In brewed coffee, we did not know who should own the timer. And no matter who did, the partner's first job was still the customer, not the timer. Conflicts still occurred.

The Better Way to make Frappuccino included a new recipe with a premade liquid base that reduced the number of steps required. But if a latte was in queue ahead of a Frappuccino—which still took longer to make—baristas would begin the more time-consuming drink first. Beverages would be finished outside of the ordering sequence, leading to disgruntled customers who felt left behind. And if a second barista came to help, they might grab cups out of the queue and further mess up the first barista's sequence.

Every Better Way led us to the next problem and to thousands of solutions being created for those problems all around the country. Over the next two years, we made small changes, adopted some practices, and rejected others.

Still, it was difficult to make these Better Ways stick. We had learned a lot about how to observe and improve work, but we still did not know what we did not know: how to create an environment around the work that supported a standardized routine.

Introducing the Playbook

In February 2011, my boss called with news that Starbucks' corporate lean team in Seattle had a brand-new answer. Instead of best practices and isolated pockets of improvement, they had created a total operating system for the stores based on lean principles. Would I be interested in helping to lead the rollout?

I'm not sure that my boss, Zeta Smith, senior vice president for the East division, was able to get the question completely out of her mouth before I said, "Absolutely. Yes."

"I don't have all the details yet," Zeta said.

"That's OK. I'm in."

There were three reasons for my enthusiasm. Ernesto's family was one of them.

For two years, people in our stores had been diligently trying to implement the Better Ways that were developed by the lean team. But every work-process innovation resulted in a dozen new problems to solve, and some of our solutions were inevitably in conflict with other Better Ways. I believed fervently that we needed something to improve operations and serve more people. And I believed in the logic and rationale of lean. But something was seriously missing.

We always seemed to be pushing solutions onto frontline leaders—the store managers, assistant managers, and supervisors—instead of engaging them in thinking through the problems. Some solutions, such as the scheduling software, were prepackaged and came with a specific set of instructions. There was little room for addressing local issues. We were expected to change our ways in order to accommodate the solution.

The Better Ways were an improvement in that they came with training in lean concepts and addressed problems that had been observed in the field. Leaders were taught to go see problems, to observe and collect data. But the solutions were still delivered to store managers instead of being arrived at by them.

I thought this was the biggest disconnect: when we changed how partners were supposed to work, the changes inevitably created new problems. This should have been an opportunity to teach problem-solving skills. But we were still learning, as leaders, how to support and guide problem solving.

I knew that members of our lean team had spent long weeks working through experiments in stores in Portland, Oregon, and Petaluma, California, so I was hopeful that this new operating system would address real-world problems. But I was wary, too, after years of watching disconnects between central operations in Seattle and stores throughout the country.

And then there was Ernesto, his wife, Carmen, and their two adorable daughters. I had just met them in January, while working on their backyard farm in Terazu, Costa Rica, plucking deep red coffee cherries off the branches of trees planted under banana trees on a steep hill. It was hard work and illuminating.

I was in Terazu with about two dozen other Starbucks leaders and agronomists,[5] getting to know more about the origins of coffee. Ernesto and Carmen had graciously welcomed us to their home— even patiently waiting while every last one of us used their only bathroom after a long bus ride.

Then they told us the story of their seven-acre farm. Years ago, Starbucks scientists had helped them increase their yields while eliminating their reliance on chemicals. Ernesto learned to better

5. Agronomy is the science of growing plants for food, fuel, and land reclamation.

balance the soil's nitrogen levels, planted those shady banana trees, and developed a lifelong partnership with Starbucks.

Over the next few days, we picked coffee cherries and put them through a pulping machine to remove the fruit from the seed. The seeds then went into a fermentation tank for a day or two to remove the slick mucilage from the seed's parchment layer. The seeds were rinsed, dried in the sun for about a week, and packed for shipping. We raked seeds on the drying beds, visited the collectives where backyard farmers sold their beans, and tasted a lot of coffee.

Farmers like Ernesto and Carmen staked their family's future on the quality of their beans. But they could not deliver that quality alone. They entrusted us to roast, grind, and brew their hard work—to deliver on what they began. I came home from that Costa Rica trip determined to make sure we did everything we could to deliver on our promise to that family and others around the globe.

A few weeks later, I was sitting alongside my colleague Steve Bremmer, a regional director from Chicago, in a Seattle head-quarters lab waiting for an introduction to the lean operating system they were calling Playbook. Looking over my shoulder, it felt like, were about a hundred store managers, baristas, and coffee farmers who were all depending on us to fix things.

Josh Howell described how we were going to bring all the Better Ways together. In the end, he said, we would understand the time it took to do the work properly and then use a formula to help us decide the right number of people to deploy for every shift. We could make work better for our frontline partners and deliver better coffee if we did it right. It was a tall order, and some of those folks looking over my shoulder were not entirely convinced.

* * *

Step one to learning this system was more lean training. We started by making a picture of work that occurred in the stores. With graph paper, rulers, and pencils—and using the data the lean team had been collecting for months—we broke down every task into timed components. We drew familiar work sequences such as brewed coffee. Next to that, we included the work of warming sandwiches, preparing an oatmeal breakfast, creating a blended drink, etc. We color-coded the sequences, using red for machine time and blue for people time.

We had drawn work sequences before, but this was different. Now, we were looking at all the interconnecting work of everyone in a store, the way it really happens. In fact, the illustration below was based on POS data collected from a Starbucks cash register in Chicago, plus time and motion studies conducted by the lean team.

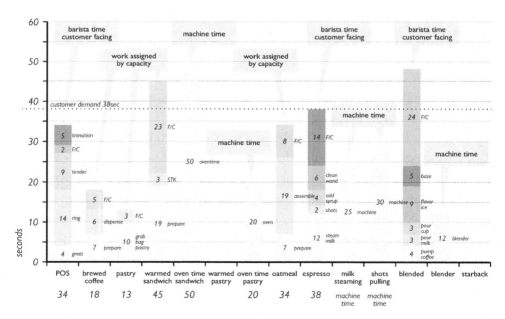

A visual picture of a store's work

We were not isolating one task, looking at it like it existed in an idealized place of no interruptions, and then trying to shave off a few seconds of time. We were looking at work by how much time it took on average to complete within a real environment, as well as the rate of customer demand. If we knew these two things, as well as who was accomplishing what tasks, we would be able to balance the work and decide how many people were needed to do what jobs.

Just having this POS data from our stores—knowing the number of pastries and brewed coffee that were ordered in a half-hour period on a weekday afternoon or weekend morning—was a huge shift in perspective. It was like taking off a very dirty pair of glasses, cleaning them, and putting them back on your face. It was amazing to me how blind we had been before this.

After we spent two hours learning how to break down work into components and then build a story of customer demand, we were ready to see how we might use this information to make staffing decisions—including how many people on each shift and everyone's roles in 30-minute increments throughout the day. The lean team referred to these decisions as "calling the play."

Think of a coach on the sidelines with a binder full of tactical plays. Based on the circumstances on the field (the strengths of the players, the weather, the opposing team, etc.) coaches will choose specific plays that they think the team will execute well. The idea was to make store managers and shift supervisors into those coaches by teaching them how to assess the field and create their own plays.

I suppose that the lean team could have created a bunch of plays based upon common circumstances and given us those instead of teaching us how to write our own. But I am glad they did not. Our stores could be radically different from one another. Some were drive-through stores off major highways with steady, near-constant demand; some stores were for commuters and had big spikes in traffic; others were community stores that relied on personal attention and community building and had many micro spikes and valleys in demand throughout the day.

That meant our managers had very different daily and weekly rhythms. They needed to know how to staff their stores for typical days and then be able to rewrite plays for atypical days when there was road construction, bad weather, a local epidemic of the flu, or a tragedy like Newtown. They needed to know how to change up staff roles when two buses full of teenagers on a field trip pulled up out front wanting Frappuccinos. Plus, managers needed to know how to write a play so that they could teach it all—theory and practice—to new leaders in training.

In the past, store managers had been taught to rely on historical sales data—presented as a six-week average and then entered into a Starbucks software program—to tell them how many baristas to have on shift at any given time. The staffing answer came, essentially, from a black box. If the store were teetering on the brink of needing six baristas on Saturday morning instead of five, the manager would not know this and could not prepare for a possible imbalance of demand to capacity.

Also, store managers had been relying on experience and intuition when it came to assigning roles within a shift. If the store sometimes had lines of customers out the door or a clear imbalance of workload between the barista and the floater, who was to say where the fault lay? Maybe this barista just wasn't as quick as others. With POS data showing customer demand and product mix, store managers would have a more complete picture about how the work of each shift might unfold.

For instance, let's say that one of our stores in rural Connecticut usually sold 120 brewed coffees and 60 espresso beverages from 8 to 8:30 a.m. on a weekday morning. From 9 to 9:30 a.m., however, that same store sold 50 brewed and 30 espressos. They needed one barista on the bar at 9 a.m., but 1.5 baristas an hour earlier at 8 a.m. So, where do we get another half a barista?

For a few weeks before our meeting, Josh, Holly, and Scott had been working on this problem with a couple of local Seattle baristas. Together, they broke down the work of baristas, cashiers, and floaters and then built standardized work routines for everyone that would allow people, when needed, to work at faster cycle times because they had fewer components to their jobs.

Prior to this, store partners did a lot of ad hoc work. If milk ran out, the barista would get a new gallon or ask the cashier to get it for them. If the cashier had time, they would usually be warming sandwiches or performing a dozen other "fetch" activities, besides taking orders. This was fine until orders went from about one every 60 seconds to one every 20 seconds.

The solution had to do with focus and interconnected work. In the new standardized routine, when a store entered a rush hour, the shift supervisor or manager would call for a new play. For this hour, the barista might work the two-beverages-at-once cycle described in A Better Way. They would remain focused only on that task. The cashier would focus solely on greeting customers, then taking orders and money—no warming sandwiches or restocking.

The floater was renamed *store support* and given new standardized work. They would make brewed coffee every eight minutes, replenish supplies for the barista and cashier based on simple visual cues, and take on many of the cashier's fetch duties, all in a repeated routine.

It sounded good in theory. But how would it play out? The lean team brought us into the lab—a full-scale mock-up of a store—and introduced us to the local baristas they had been working with. Using POS data from one of Steve's very busy downtown Chicago stores, they began sending people through the line with orders at a real-world, rush-hour clip.

I stationed myself at the espresso bar to watch the action and almost immediately fell into a conversation with the barista. Starbucks had recently come out with a new benefits package, and I liked asking our partners what they thought of it. She and I chatted about benefits and such while she worked steadily through her line of cups, producing one beverage after another. When she ran low on whole milk, she threw the red cap off the gallon of milk into a clear plexiglass cube and returned to her measured two-beverage cadence. The support partner collected the replenishment signals out of the Plexiglas cube about three minutes later and then returned with the gallon of milk.

After 15 minutes, the demonstration ended, and I looked up in surprise. The barista—working at a much faster pace than normal—had been chatting with me the entire time. I asked how she managed to do that, and she smiled. "I'm just doing this one thing," she said. "I can work faster when I keep my focus."

In fact, everyone could work more efficiently while single-tasking for a definable period, such as a morning rush. After the rush was over, the shift supervisor could call a new play and give everyone a chance to move around in a different way.

I was convinced.

* * *

However, turning around and convincing 10 district managers and 110 store managers of the necessity of this change was going to be another matter. One of the more difficult things to do is convince people to set aside their own intuition and experience and adopt a new routine. I knew that before beginning the spread of Playbook.

Still, I believed this system would make work substantially better for our frontline leaders. So, I selected two district managers, David and Jen, and together we selected one "seed store" from each of their areas. Our initial idea was to train the store managers in some lean thinking tools and the Playbook methods and then have them train their supervisors. The assistant store manager and supervisors would then train the rest of the staff. This was a kind of learn-do-teach routine that we had used successfully in the past. Only this time, everyone needed more theory and background.

For David and Jen, and store managers Courtney and Suzie, training began in Seattle, where they could visit the lab and see the target state, run by well-trained baristas. Their stores would function as labs for other stores in New England, so it was important that they saw a great example. They learned how to build work stories—breaking down each job into all of its timed components—and how to move components of one job to another job, when necessary. They learned how to use POS data and build their plays for half-hour segments throughout a day. Together we built training plans for the weeks ahead.[6]

And then Courtney and Suzie returned home to Connecticut to two very different stores. Courtney's store in West Hartford was very near a university and served a diverse population that was part urban community, part commuters, with a strong academic influence. There could be odd spikes in demand throughout the day, and tables were often filled with study groups and people working on laptops.

6. Starbucks is known for its professional training department. But we were working outside of the mainstream on this project, and the five of us built our own training program based on Starbucks' ideas and principles.

Suzie's store was in Westport—one of the wealthiest towns in the nation. It's an easy commute from New York City and is known for celebrities, Wall Street titans, and other success stories. The morning commute rush at that Starbucks was intensely busy, and the customers were not known for being laid back. Some partners admitted to being a little afraid of the more volatile guests.

The styles of the two store managers were completely different, too. Courtney was a collaborative leader. She was comfortable leading with questions—which frustrated some baristas—and had a good reputation for mentoring and guiding new leaders.

Suzie was more comfortable with control. Under the pressure of a commuter rush with a line of impatient guests stretching out of the door, Suzie assessed situations quickly and rapped out directions to her crew. She was more comfortable telling people what to do than seeking help and advice.

For each store, we began with an all-hands meeting to explain the new training and the reasons for change. The West Hartford meeting seemed to go quite well. After hours, the baristas pulled their chairs into a circle in the center of the café, all knees pointed to the center, and listened attentively while Courtney outlined the case for change—including the big vision, the benefits, and the resources that would be put into making it successful. People might have shifted uncomfortably in their chairs once or twice, but overall, they seemed willing to try this new operating system.

Westport was a different story. When Suzie asked her staff to gather, they dragged their chairs a little closer, but not much. Some of them sat facing away from each other, arms crossed, and asked hard questions about how this would affect their work and their customers. Suzie did not spend as much time talking about the benefits of the new system.

Still, both stores began training toward the change. Courtney and Suzie trained their assistant managers and shift supervisors in three specific modules: 5S,[7] kanban,[8] and creating plays from POS data. In turn, these leaders selected a group of partners to learn together. These were groups of three—called training pods—composed of people who generally worked together. The assistant store manager might take charge of training pods of day-shift partners, while a shift supervisor who worked evenings would take evening pods. That way, partners could work through what they learned together.

After learning about 5S, groups cleaned and organized the storeroom, kitchen, and counter area. Learning about kanban systems meant choosing replenishment signals to put in an easily seen clear plexiglass cube, such as the red cap off a gallon of whole milk or a plastic hot-beverage lid with green tape to indicate the need for 20 medium hot to-go cups. Learning groups also worked through sample plays, learning to switch from one role to another, and memorized the store-support work sequence.

Using our learn-do-teach routine, a shift supervisor would teach a barista the tasks of store support, have the barista perform one or two cycles as the store-support partner, and still have time in a shift to have that barista turn around and teach someone else the role of store support. We did it this way because it is always easier to remember a job's key points and rationale for doing tasks in a particular order when you have taught it to someone else.

We trained our partners and worked out kinks for two months in our first two stores. We fretted over every detail as we got closer to our "go-live" dates. What we did not do was prepare our customers.

7. Popularized by the Toyota Production System and based on five Japanese words that begin with S; 5S focuses on cleaning, organizing, and standardizing the workplace.
8. A system for replenishing stock based on signals.

Remember that Starbucks' goal was to connect with customers. Most stores had a population of daily or twice-daily customers. We knew their names and their favorite drinks, and to make them feel special, we often started making their drink when they walked in the door or even when their car pulled into the parking lot.

Or a barista would call down the line of customers, "Hey, Marge! Is it a latte or a mocha today?" Beverages were started out of order on a regular basis.

The problem with this friendly anarchy is that we needed to use customer buildup in front of the barista bar as a visual alert for when demand was outrunning capacity. For the signal to be accurate, we needed to make drinks in the same sequence as the ordering. Now just imagine if three strangers ordered drinks right ahead of four regulars—a not uncommon occurrence. The three strangers would be marooned in front of the bar, waiting and watching, while the regulars' drinks got made first. Their presence would throw off a false signal. So, we told baristas to stop making drinks out of order for favorite customers.

Some of our regulars were not happy. While I was observing the action one morning in Westport, a customer stalked across the café and yelled at me that I needed to leave the baristas alone and let them do their jobs. (In this case, he meant, beginning work on his venti extra-dry cappuccino the minute he walked in the door.)

So, David, Jen, and I took up positions in the seed stores, explaining to customers what we were doing and handing out free-coffee cards to disgruntled customers. We agreed that once we started on this road, we would not fall back to our old ways. We would make apologies, problem solve, and keep moving ahead.

Also, I expected these two very different stores to have dissimilar issues with the changes. They were very different to begin with. What was interesting—for those of us who are fascinated with change management—is how and when the problems became apparent in these stores.

Remember that Courtney in West Hartford was a collaborative leader and loathed to give answers. Her team had problems early on—before the Playbook launch—when they needed to decide on storewide replenishment signals.

The evening shift team, while learning about kanban, would suggest one signal for "need 10 tall cold drink cups." The day shift team would have a slightly different answer. Instead of choosing one and moving on, Courtney might encourage the two teams to dialogue about it. But schedules would not match up, meetings were suggested and delayed, decisions dragged out. As we got closer to the planned go-live date for the new operating system, some partners in this store became nervous. They asked for more time and said they would never be ready. But really, they just needed to agree on their replenishment signals.

Meanwhile, Suzie in Westport had everything well in hand until after Playbook was launched. Accustomed to rapping out directions on the fly during a rush hour, she had a hard time sticking to the agreed-upon plays. For instance, pastry replenishment would be part of the regular duties of the store-support partner. But if Suzie saw that pastries needed replenishing while she was working the cash register, she would simply go do that—sometimes leaving a new customer to confront an empty counter while throwing a support partner off their routine. Her tendency to arrive at and announce solutions quickly meant the other partners were not learning how to problem solve. Before long, Suzie's staff members were in open rebellion about the way rules and roles were getting changed mid-rush. After some retraining and personal attention from her district manager, Suzie got much better at following plays.

We learned a lot from those first two stores. We took those lessons and chose 10 more stores for beta sites—one for each district manager, including a second store each for David and Jen. This time, we set up a 10-week cycle for store managers, supervisors, and baristas, including time for training, to go live, and then to stabilize. Then we took a short breather and chose another 10 stores—this time moving through the launch cycle in just eight weeks.

It kept us focused and gave us a lot of experience working through the lean problem-solving process. In fact, problem solving was steadily becoming part of everyone's job.

Let Me Fix That For You

Before we began working with a lean operating system, the problem solver was usually the highest-ranking leader in the room. If we knew about a problem, we took action to fix it. That was the job of a leader, and we were proud of that role.

Let's say that a store in Manchester, Connecticut, was off-plan in the sale of peppermint lattes. Maybe we had decided they should be able to sell 75 every day in December, but they were selling only 50. If a district manager noticed the problem, it was their job to find a solution.

Some district managers might take the "go-see" approach and try to gather information on why sales were under the target. But others found questions like, "Why do you think you're not selling peppermint lattes?" to be too confrontational. It was easier to offer solutions than to put a person on the spot.

So, the district manager would pick up the phone, call the store manager, and say something like, "I see that you're off-plan on peppermint lattes. Let's make sure we give out 200 samples a day and push those sales higher."

Most of us leaders assumed that, with more experience and a global view of the situation, we were better equipped to provide answers. None of us would have dreamed of leaving problems in the lap of our direct report. It was our job to fix it for them.

But then we were introduced to scientific methods and the plan-do-check-adjust (PDCA) cycle of experimentation and problem solving. It was like a light went on. That light was on a dimmer and came up slowly over a year or so, but it did turn on because PDCA was really more in line with our people-centric culture.

Back in the early and mid-2000s, under the leadership of Howard Behar, most of the regional managers and executives attended seminars in servant leadership, and I, for one, really embraced the idea. We learned that our role was to facilitate the success of others and I wanted to achieve that. But how could we facilitate that success when we were always telling people what to do? Was giving instructions the same thing as coaching? There was a deep disconnect at first.

Then we started to learn about A3 thinking, and a glimmer of light came through. This was a method of working through problems together instead of throwing solutions at people. It was more like teamwork. It certainly made me feel more vulnerable, which is what you were supposed to feel as a servant leader. But I wasn't really sure how working through an A3 would facilitate the success of others.

It was during the rollout of Playbook that all of these elements came together for me. A lean operating system is really good at exposing problems. They come up immediately and frequently. But it was no longer leadership's role to fix those problems. We could not possibly fix them all since we could not be on the front line of work every moment of every day. It was our job, we were told, to coach people through their own problem solving.

In general, the frontline problems being uncovered were not big, intractable problems; they were the kind of daily annoyances that interrupted workflows. Using an A3 required a great deal of coaching and seemed too large a hammer for the nails being uncovered. So, instead of an A3, we almost always used a simple PDCA problem-solving cycle.

For instance, let's say a seasonal latte just came out requiring caramel syrup. If the store did not have a replenishment signal for caramel syrup, the barista was going to run into a problem when the syrup ran out. This could be solved immediately by asking the store-support partner for syrup, or the barista could run and get it. But for an enduring solution, in which everyone in the store would have an agreed-upon signal for caramel-syrup replenishment, the barista would need to engage all the partners. To do this, the barista would put a note on the problem board we set up in every store's office. The problem boards explained the problem-solving cycle:

Plan: State the problem and a proposed countermeasure.

Do: Put the countermeasure in action.

Check: Revisit the problem to see if the countermeasure works.

Adjust: Train others and make it the standard.

The problem-solving cycle

1. **identify the problem**
   (difference between where you want to be and where you are)

2. **observe and measure current state**
   (go see: collect facts)

3. **set a goal**
   (measured target of what should happen)

4. **write a problem statement**
   (clear concise description of gap)

5. **analyze the gap**
   (what, why, why not)

6. **select & test countermeasures**

7. **check results**

8. **adjust plan**

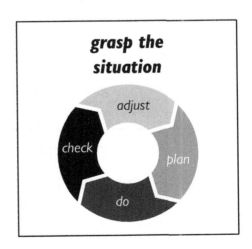

There were areas on the board to pin up problems currently moving through PDCA, as well as new issues like the replenishment signal for that caramel syrup. Full team meetings are difficult to have in most Starbucks stores due to the the differing shifts. But shift supervisors held brief meetings in front of the board to discuss and resolve issues at the beginning of shifts. That meant people could post and agree upon new replenishment signals, as well as delve into larger issues, such as unsold breakfast sandwiches.

In many ways, the issue of underwhelming sales on breakfast sandwiches—specifically, the sausage and egg on an English muffin—was much like those peppermint lattes, in that the problem first became clear in the sales spreadsheet of a district manager. This district manager knew she should not simply tell the store manager what to do. Instead, she mentored the store manager through the PDCA process.

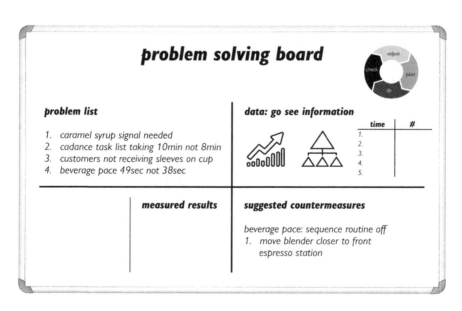

Problem-solving notes for caramel syrup signal

The first step in solving a problem is to go see it. So, the district manager visited the store and coached the store manager through the problem-solving process with questions like, "How can we set up a way to see this problem?"

Because the first question around any consumable product is whether people like it, the store manager suggested setting up a sampling. During the morning rush, they asked the store support partners to heat up, cut up, and hand out breakfast sandwiches to people waiting to order. The results came back immediately: sandwiches were handed back with the complaint that they were still cold in the middle.

Cold? The store manager reheated a sandwich using the right oven settings and time and found the same result: cold in the middle. They reheated other types of sandwiches using the called-for settings and found them to be just right. So, the problem was only with the sausage and egg sandwich.

In problem-solving meetings at the beginning of shift, groups considered the mystery: why was only one type of sandwich cold in the middle? Countermeasures were proposed and attempted, but nothing made sense until someone checked the stacks of sandwiches thawing in the refrigerator. When every other sandwich was thawed and ready for reheating, only the sausage English muffins that were stacked vertically were still frozen in the center. But sausage muffins stacked flat for thawing were fine. So, if they got jumbled on a tray and the stacks fell over, or a bunch of sausage sandwiches were in a box turned on its side, they did not thaw right. A district manager, visiting the store once every two weeks, would not have been able to uncover this root cause.

With that mystery solved, the store manager returned to step 1 of their plan and resampled the sandwiches during morning rush. Customers liked them, and sales rebounded. For the final "adjust" phase of the PDCA process, a sign was put on the refrigerator to remind partners to lay all sandwiches flat for thawing.

This story also reveals a bit of our management system in action. In order to escalate problems that needed more attention and to coach our direct reports through addressing their problems, we had a series of regularly scheduled meetings that linked together.

Once every two weeks, district managers met personally with store managers and—after a coffee tasting, of course—reviewed problems that were being addressed through PDCA. Once a month, I would meet with all of my district managers individually to coach them through their own problems, plus help with any store issues that needed intervention at my level.

For instance, when a district manager was having a difficult time illustrating the visual standards for "clean floor" and "not clean" across several stores, I was able to provide help from a regional quality assurance partner who created a book with clearly pictured examples, and instructions in the use of the special soap for floors.

Another issue that quickly came to the surface had to do with how fast and focused some of the jobs had become. Some baristas and cashiers complained of repetitive stress after two hours or more during a rush, and it was clear that the store-support role could be exhausting. It was a problem that could not be solved at the store or district level, yet it needed local countermeasures.

Working with partners in our initial seed stores, we soon found that people were happier and had much fewer complaints about repetitive stress if they knew that a play was running on a clock. If the fast, focused work was for a 60- or 90-minute cycle, after which time they could be moved into a different role, partners felt less stress. Some people wanted to stay in the same role through fast and slow periods, while others craved the change. Shift supervisors learned to move people or not, based on partner preferences.

Knowing that we needed to move people into different roles frequently also made us more deliberate about cross-training. Instead of cross-training when opportunities presented themselves, district managers began coaching new stores to schedule cross-training while their store partners were learning about 5S and kanban. It became part of a store's preparation for Playbook.

Cross-training, we also found, was actually easier now because every job had a very specific set of tasks and a rhythm. It was much easier to learn a job where B always followed A versus a job with instructions like, "If you run out of milk, there should be more in the back refrigerator, but you don't want to leave your espresso machine during rush hour."

As 10 stores running Playbook became 30 stores and then 50, I learned a lot about leading the spread of a lean operating system. Being close to the store-level rollout in those first few weeks was essential, especially for my own understanding. I knew all the baristas in Westport and West Hartford and had considered their different working and communication styles. I thought a lot about how to manage them and shared my thoughts with my district managers, as well as the store managers.

So, when issues came up with a new store in the second or third set of rollouts, I was inclined to dive right in, asking the district manager how the shift supervisor or store manager was problem solving and what specific steps had been taken. This led to messages being carried back and forth and muddied waters. My involvement too often made people in the chain of command stop what they were doing and wait for an answer from me. This was counterproductive.

I learned to focus instead on asking questions about the steps being taken by my direct report. Limiting my coaching—mostly—to the district manager meant all communication was direct, causing fewer misunderstandings, and kept the district manager empowered to coach store managers. Repositioning my role meant I was focusing my energy on the growth of my district managers, which is exactly as it should be.

* * *

As the summer of 2012 ended, we had crossed the threshold of more than half of New England stores converted to the Playbook. And we were seeing some benefits. Productivity was inching upward. In stores running the Playbook, we were moving up from 10 or 11 transactions per labor hour to 12 or 13. It was a big deal on the spreadsheets to improve the profitability of labor. We were not using fewer people; we were selling more. As our partners were able to perform more transactions per hour, we created better cash flow.

Still, our spreadsheets were not the big emotional win that we could use to sell new stores on the need for this change.[9] It was not easy to convince partners that the hard work of reforming their habits was worth a point or two of productivity.

Then came Black Friday at the Holyoke Mall in Massachusetts. If you have never worked retail on the day after Thanksgiving—the biggest shopping day of the year in the United States—it is difficult to describe the mix of adrenaline and dread that comes with preparing for Black Friday. It is not just that there are four or five times as many shoppers as usual. They are also distracted by their lists, harried by all the other shoppers, and desperately in need of some eggnog-fueled holiday cheer.

---

9. It is important to note that Playbook was being introduced as an experiment only in two regions—Chicago and New England. We needed to show what the lean operating system could and could not do.

So, they come to Starbucks. On the average Friday, registers in one of our mall stores tallied up about 615 transactions. On Black Friday, transactions jumped to 3,000. Every year, we planned for the day as if for an invasion. I collected sandwich orders for the partners in all of the mall stores in my region—tuna fish for Holyoke, peanut butter and jelly for Stamford, Connecticut—and made dozens of sandwiches in my kitchen before heading out to deliver them beginning at 4 a.m. like some deli-based Kris Kringle.

Store managers like Carol Ann at Holyoke began their planning weeks in advance: ordering ingredients and supplies in massive quantities, giving personal training to any partner who had not yet worked Black Friday, making sure that all hands were on deck. Carol Ann was always available, day or night, to her store staff, and she usually worked far too much in the days leading up to Black Friday. Her system always got that store through the crisis in the past, but they were running a different system now: Playbook.

Then one of Carol Ann's shift supervisors, Ryan, asked whether he could lead the store on Black Friday. He was well trained and had been successfully calling plays and running operations without Carol Ann on premises for a number of months, but the request was still a surprise. This was Black Friday we were talking about. It was like a tsunami of people. Still, we needed to test Playbook.

Carol Ann and Ryan talked about plans before Black Friday, of course. But Carol Ann also made a sincere effort to spend less time at work, to trust the system to do its job. On the day after Thanksgiving that year, she showed up at her regular time. She made sure all the baristas showed up and that the bathrooms were clean, and then she watched in awe as Ryan pulled off a nearly flawless day.

In order to keep partners focused on one job at a time, Ryan had decided to eliminate one of the blenders. He had studied the POS data and the workflow and was convinced that eliminating a blender would help baristas remain in the right work routine, at the right pace. We all held our breath, but the POS data had told the truth, and one blender easily accommodated all the Frappuccinos that were ordered. At the end of the day, the store at Holyoke Mall broke all previous sales records—with just one blender.

We finally had the story that we could tell store managers about why they needed to convert to the Playbook: The manager of one of the busiest stores in New England could now take scheduled days off—in a row—without getting frantic phone calls from the store. Playbook was not just a new kind of work routine. If Carol Ann could let a shift supervisor run the store on Black Friday, Playbook could be a kind of freedom for all of us. We just needed everyone on board.

* * *

All evidence to the contrary, I suppose it is human nature to think that change will eventually stop. We make changes and then make improvements to those changes; everyone learns their roles, we all agree that it's better, and then things will just stay that way, right? Even if we are prepared for a certain amount of backsliding, it is still disappointing when the operating system that everyone agreed was better frays around the edges.

I noticed it first in the lower-volume stores. Partners who weren't stressed out by the old ad hoc work methods had a hard time memorizing new routines. If they didn't actually need to work twice as fast for two-hour periods three times a day, they could easily forget why they needed a partner in the store-support role. The shift supervisor then might go back to making coffee (occasionally) and restocking the drinks cooler instead of calling plays and coaching.

And the store-support person, thrown off routine by half of their job being taken away, would begin wandering off path and forgetting things. I was ready for that and coached my district managers to set up regular audit visits in order to coach store managers when partners were out of sync.

What I was not prepared for was backsliding at big stores that had been helped enormously by Playbook. Sometime after Black Friday, I stopped in at the Holyoke Mall store and was surprised to see the store-support partner—I could tell what her role was because she was wearing the little brewed-coffee timer clipped to her apron—reach up and casually reset the timer for another minute when it went off instead of going to make more coffee. It was not terribly busy in the store, but she was helping the barista make espresso drinks. I was not sure who the play caller was.

We had proved that the synchronized, standardized work routines of Playbook helped everyone get their job done without scurrying and stress. Why would people drop the routine?

Sometimes hiccups from Seattle got in the way of our lean operating system. Every store manager received regular promotional books from Seattle with instructions on how to promote new products or accomplish certain tasks. Best-practices memos sometimes gave directions that contradicted the Playbook system— a problem that was only in Chicago and New England at that time. And district managers did not always follow up on problems reported by store managers, so issues went unresolved and became barriers to getting people back into synchronized routines.

Still, we kept rolling that boulder up the hill. We worked through problems, coached partners on their roles, and planned to move more stores to the Playbook system. We had seen it work, so we thought we knew its power.

We did not know the half of it.

Steady Work

The Worst Week Ever

The worst week ever did not begin the way I thought it might. There was no smell of sulfur, no odd light in the morning sky. There was a text message on my phone: *Have you seen the news?*

I switched on the television and think I heard only the first few sentences. There had been a shooting at an elementary school in Newtown, Connecticut. There were a lot of casualties. Children killed. Other children, terrified, running hand in hand across a lawn.

It was like a bell jar had dropped over my head. I live in Connecticut and have four sons. I could not hear what they were saying on television while I did that mental inventory that I think every parent does. My eldest son, recently graduated from college, was at work. Two more sons were in high school, on campus. My husband, Brian, had already packed our youngest son's lunch, double-checked his backpack, and driven him to our local elementary school that was a hundred miles from Sandy Hook Elementary. Brian was now back home; I could see him in the backyard with the dog.

I could breathe.

And then I flipped into emergency planning. This was just a few weeks after Superstorm Sandy had slammed the East Coast, running hard up the Long Island Sound and flooding parts of southern Connecticut. I knew how people gravitated toward our cafés in a crisis. For days, people had been without power in some parts of the state after Sandy hit. No refrigeration for milk or food, no electricity for cell phones. Starbucks stores across the region had been packed and supply chains stretched thin. The memories were fresh.

I sent a text to one of my district managers, asking him to alert other district managers and meet me in Newtown. Driving south, I did a mental assessment of the store. It was next to a Catholic church and school, about a mile and a half from Sandy Hook Elementary School. I doubted the store would be shut down by the police crime scene perimeter.

Newtown was a community store with a lot of tables in the café. But the supply room was so small; it was hardly bigger than a closet. People were always talking about how to work within its confines, how to organize it for maximum efficiency. The store's refrigerator was unreliable, I remembered.

All the way down the Yankee Expressway I drove, letting my mind fill with logistical details. Newtown had converted over to the Playbook system about four months earlier, and they seemed to be doing well. The store manager—David B., in his early 40s with plenty of experience—was very positive about how people were adapting. But did they have enough baristas? We might need to fill in partner vacancies from stores around the state. We might need extra supplies sooner than our regular delivery. When southern Connecticut had flooded, our stores had run out of food fast.

I called my boss, Zeta, from the road and she began notifying leaders in Seattle. Then I made mental lists about whom to call for additional resources. In this way, I kept myself from thinking about what happened for about an hour and a half. I thought I was prepared.

Newtown is one of those small New England towns with a lot more trees than people. Old rocky farms have been reverting to forestland for more than a hundred years. White pine, oak, and hickory trees have filled in where open fields once stood. Sugar maple trees and yellow birch are the big showstoppers in autumn when their leaves go bright orange, red, and yellow.

As I pulled off the highway, I could see that nearly all of that natural color was gone and people were massing everywhere. The big church parking lot next door to Starbucks was filling with cars and news vans bristling with antennae. The grassy slope in front of the Starbucks—normally empty and unused—was dotted with knots of people. The store's parking lot was filled to overflowing, and there were more people walking over from the church.

I knew from the radio that the gunman was dead at the scene. They believed he was acting alone. But seeing all those people out on the streets in this normally quiet town set my nerves on high alert.

Inside the Starbucks, four baristas and David were working fast to keep up with the rush, and their faces were all like stones. Seeing that shock had set in, I met first on the sidelines with Emily, the incoming manager for that district of 10 stores. Recently a store manager herself, we asked her to talk with David and the partners individually to see whether anyone needed to go home.

While none of the partners had victims in their immediate families that day, this was a small town and a close-knit community. We knew that everyone would be affected somehow, would be grieving for neighbors, cousins, favorite teachers. Soon, we would learn that 20 children—all six or seven years old—and six staff members of the school were killed that morning. It was too much for anyone to process.

None of the partners wanted to go home right away. Customers kept streaming in the door. Two more baristas arrived for their regular afternoon shifts. The out-going district manager, Bethany, got on the phone to check the status of partners throughout the area and see about getting extra help in Newtown.

Starbucks stores all receive regular deliveries from company trucks a few times a week. Newtown was not due to receive more food until the next day, and that delivery—having been ordered four days earlier—was only enough food for a normal weekend. I asked another district manager to track down extra pastries and sandwiches at stores around the state. We sent another team member out to pick them up. We filled travelers with coffee and sent them to the first responders.

As the afternoon became evening, new waves of people showed up. They came from prayer vigils at the church, from community meetings being held all over town. Members of the press arrived with microphones and cameras, trying to snag people for interviews while they waited for coffee. As politely as I could, I sent them outside.

Bethany found many willing partners from around the district to help in the Newtown store but was troubled by one absence. She could not find Lauren Rousseau, a 30-year-old barista and substitute teacher who worked in one of the Danbury stores about 20 minutes down the highway. Lauren's sister, Emily, worked in the Bristol store; Emily had called to say that her family had not heard from Lauren.

It is difficult to remember much of that evening. I know that it seemed quiet in the store, despite the steady stream of people coming and going. There were no dramas behind the counter, no emergencies. Families came in and sat ashen-faced around tables. Baristas started delivering orders to the tables. It just seemed wrong to shout out names for beverage pickup that night.

We all cleaned and closed the store together. I drove home late with the news playing on the radio. Officials said they would release the names of the dead at 8 a.m. the next morning. At home, I checked in on my sleeping boys and started preparing for what would probably be a worse day tomorrow.

At 8 a.m. that Saturday, I was parked outside the Danbury store when they released the names of the dead. Lauren Rousseau was among them. I walked into the store and Hester, the store manager, took one look at my face and knew, she told me later. I went around and asked customers to please take their orders to go; we were closing the store. And then we were locking the doors, putting out a sign, and asking the partners to gather around.

Most of them knew that Lauren wasn't working day shifts during the week anymore, not since she had finally landed a permanent teaching job at Sandy Hook Elementary, just a few weeks earlier. It was entry level, but it fulfilled the dream she worked so hard for.

Lauren was born just up the road at Danbury Hospital. She had been working with us since just after completing her master's degree at the University of Bridgeport. She was inquisitive and cheerful; everyone liked working with her. She was working with us when she fell in love with the man she might have married and when she got her first teaching jobs. We did not expect we would be able to keep her much longer, but we thought we would have been able to say goodbye.

All that morning, behind the locked doors of the café, we talked about Lauren. I brought in lunch and EAP counselors,[10] and we told stories of the things Lauren said or did. We cried and didn't cry; we talked and didn't talk. We created a space to begin to process all of the loss that was around us. In the afternoon, we packed up all of the store's sandwiches and pastries into a couple of cars and drove to Newtown.

The Newtown store was even busier than the day before. During an average week, partners in Newtown usually rang up about 4,000 transactions. The Danbury store—conveniently located and visible just off the highway—would average 6,000 transactions in a week. By closing that store, we had pushed even more traffic through Newtown. During the morning rush, Newtown baristas usually

10. Employee Assistance Program

produced 70 espresso beverages. On this Saturday morning, it had been about 240. And everyone was hungry. Instead of ordering one or two coffees, most of the transactions had double the number of drinks and added pastries and sandwiches.

While others packed all the food from Danbury into every conceivable space we could find in the Newtown store, I checked in with Emily and David and looked over the operating plays they were building. Since the store was seeing demand like never before, we had only the previous day's POS data to guide us. That was enough to see that we now needed 10 partners: two baristas on espresso drinks, two people on the cash register, two cash register support partners, and four store-support partners.

The cashiers' duties were to greet people, ring up transactions, and take money. Cashier support partners marked drink orders on cups, collected pastries, and handed off sandwiches for warming. Store-support partners made brewed coffee—a lot more coffee—and did all of their usual duties. They warmed sandwiches and kept café tables and floors clean. They washed dishes, helped deliver beverages to guests when time allowed, cleaned bathrooms, and kept all the cases stocked with food. These were the same off-line and replenishment duties the support partner had always done; there were just more of them.

When problems arose, partners could solve most of them immediately, maybe with a little help from store support. Any issue that could not be easily fixed was escalated to the shift supervisor. In the illustration of a play at right, you can see a shift supervisor with the label "play caller."

The play caller was there to coach, recognize and resolve bottlenecks, and help solve problems that arose. If an order came in for six blended drinks at once, for instance, the play caller could move a store-support partner over to the blender to help out. If inventory in the pastry case was running low, the play caller would find out why replenishment was stalled and perhaps coach a partner back into the proper work sequence.

Play caller was a difficult job for many ex-baristas who were accustomed to jumping into a situation and resolving problems with their own two hands. This role required using words more than actions. In my experience, it requires more on-going training and coaching than any other role.

During these days of heightened activity, at least one or two district managers and I were also at the Newtown store, handling the issues that were unique to the time and place. Someone was always running out to deliver coffee or to pick up pastries from another store. If a table full of reporters had been dominating the café for hours, using every electrical outlet because each had two or three hungry phones, I would go out to negotiate. Mostly, I offered them directions to another nearby Starbucks.

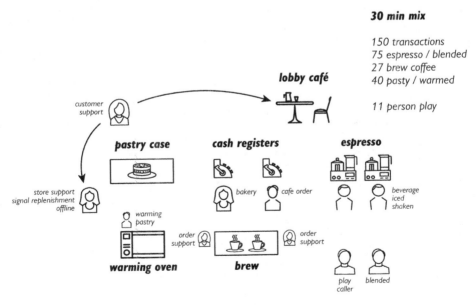

Eleven person play used at Newtown

By about 7 p.m., we could usually send a couple of partners home. At that point the play would look like the one below until closing. In the morning, we would be back to 10–12 people on shift.

And on that Sunday, I saw another remarkable development. Over the weekend, it became clear that the emotional strain was too much for some people. A few baristas opted to stay home for a day or two. David, the store manager, did not ask for time off, but we encouraged him to take a week's vacation. He gratefully accepted.

This would have been unthinkable two years earlier. Before Playbook, every store manager ran the operation to suit their own tastes. Yes, we had standards. But how work was assigned and executed, and how changes were communicated, could change a lot from one store to the next. It might take the staff months to become accustomed enough to a new manager to achieve a good working rhythm. If a store were suddenly doing triple its normal business, like Newtown was, I would never have encouraged a manager to take vacation. I probably would have hunkered down and figured out how to help him work through it.

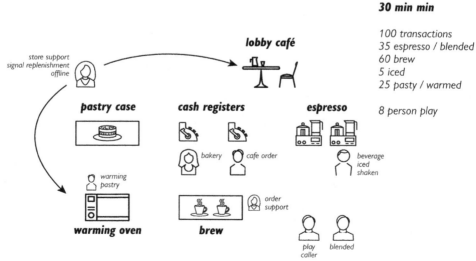

30 min min

100 transactions
35 espresso / blended
60 brew
5 iced
25 pasty / warmed

8 person play

Eight person play for Newtown close

But that Sunday—one day before the first of the funerals would be held, when there were prayer vigils every hour at the church next door, when the media presence was at its height—we were able to change store managers midstream.

Lori, the temporary store manager, did not have the same temperament as David, and she had not worked in the Newtown store before. (The tiny storeroom was certainly a shock.) But she managed another store using the Playbook methods, and so, in the most important ways, she was just like David. Lori could already communicate job assignments in fine detail with shift supervisors and knew that they were already in agreement on the meaning of POS data. It was as if this team, all meeting for the first time, was seasoned by months of common understanding.

Late on Sunday, we reopened the Danbury store, staffed by a team of baristas and supervisors from a store about 20 minutes away, just over the New York border. Their store was not operating in a Playbook system, so we trained them briefly and quickly, enabling them to work with the Danbury team members who were coming back a few at a time. We also asked a Starbucks human resources partner to take up a spot in the café and be there if needed.

Having extra hands like our HR partner proved useful very quickly. As soon as the store reopened, people from Danbury—customers, friends, former schoolmates—focused on the store as a place to go and express their grief. They dropped off flowers, teddy bears, and all sorts of little gifts in purple, which was Lauren's favorite color. They asked about scholarship funds or wanted to share their memories. Having a person there to receive gifts and be able to relate information about memorials was incredibly valuable.

In Newtown, the phone never stopped ringing. The store manager was fielding 100 calls a day instead of less than 10. People called to ask for news, to offer prayers. People called from across the country to buy gift cards, loaded with hundreds of dollars, and asked us to deliver them to overworked police officers and health care workers. Finally, one of the district managers decided that we needed an answering machine for the store, went out and bought one, and figured out how to set it up. Sitting down once every hour to listen to messages, compose answers, and return calls became part of the standardized work routine of the store manager.

On Monday morning, even with Danbury now open and taking on the regular commuter traffic, Newtown was just as busy as it had been. Or more so. The international press was everywhere, but so were other people—families from all around the state, gathering for the first of the 26 funerals and memorials. People kept talking about how small the caskets were. Emotions were raw.

Yet for many of the store's partners, work had become a respite, they told me. Outside the café, the whole world was grieving and filled with unanswerable questions. When they came to work, however, they knew exactly what to do. Their jobs were clearly defined, easily repeatable sequences. They weren't running into each other, over-lapping steps, or missing orders. A kind of calm had taken over as partners focused on their jobs and on providing some degree of comfort in a terrible time.

Tuesday and Wednesday brought more funerals, but we found that we were not so focused on the high volume of work. It had quickly become routine. Over the course of this week, we would ring up 9,000 transactions—more than double the usual pace. And the actual sales were much higher still, due to the increased volume of food and beverage sold with each order.

* * *

Looking back on it, I now realize with some surprise that I never asked for permission to carry out my decisions that week. Closing the Danbury store for a day and a half, moving a crew over from New York to fill in, dramatically increasing the number of people working shifts in the Newtown store—I informed my boss about what we were doing but never asked permission. And even though Newtown was at the center of the entire country's attention, nobody from Seattle stepped in to tell me what I should do. Howard Shultz and others called to offer assistance but not direction.

I think it is human nature for people to jump in during a crisis and try to grab the reins. In fact, I have to admit that if this had happened in a pre-Playbook time, I probably would have micromanaged everything. I certainly would have thrown a lot more people into the mix. I would not have known what the right resources were and so would have acted emotionally and erred on the side of extra help. Then I would have offered a lot of instructions for all of those baristas tripping over each other, and it probably would have been a well-meaning disaster.

Playbook worked well because it made standard work of important business decisions. As long as you followed the formulas based on the POS data and truly understood the time it took to do the work, you would have the right number of people working. And the habit of daily team-based problem solving built up our capability to handle a cascade of issues coming at us all at once.

In this case, Playbook was a champion because decisions that were difficult to make in the moment had already been made for us. When we were stressed in every way, we trusted the operating system to be our guide. Also, at no point did we have to stop and worry about whether we were making a profit. Even though we were throwing a lot of extra resources at the Newtown store, I knew that the balance sheet would work out. Balanced productivity was baked into every play.

But the most important aspect of the lean operating system was that it supported the frontline partners. In that awful week, standardized work was not a yoke; it was a comfort. It gave us breathing room. It guided us to synchronize our efforts and work as one. It took away the dozens of exhausting little decisions we make on the job and provided certainty.

The question is, why would we ever do anything else? We proved that the Playbook—or any lean operating system based on standardized work—could be a saving grace in a crisis. But when the crisis passed, people fell out of the discipline. Why?

Growth and More Growth

In the spring of 2013, we completed the transformation of all stores in my region to the Playbook lean operating system and could report impressive results. From 2008 to 2013, we recorded the following improvements in customer service, productivity, new-employee turnover, and internal promotion rates.

Overall customer satisfaction at Starbucks in my region went from 66% to 82%. This was measured by random surveys, in which paying customers were asked to go to a website and give feedback on their experience, often in return for discounts or free coffee. People were asked about the quality of the product, their experience with employees, and their overall satisfaction. We watched all the categories, but we speculated that "quality of product" responses could be driven by new latte flavors and "experience with employees" might refer more to how cute or friendly the barista was. We did pay special attention to that last question about overall satisfaction, though. This was the needle we wanted to move. The more organized, less frantic atmosphere of our stores—coupled with shorter wait times and more focused partners—was the biggest factor, I believe, in moving that overall satisfaction number.

Productivity, measured in transactions per labor hour, rose from 9.8 to 13. This translated, of course, to more money for Starbucks. Because the work was improved, it was easier to process more transactions using the same number of people. I was particularly proud of the fact that this was not desperate productivity, made by wringing more transactions out of stressed-out partners. This was quality productivity that rose because we were more effectively using the people available to us. The evidence to support this is clearly visible in the next result.

Employees who quit within the first 90 days of being hired is a closely watched metric throughout the QSR industry. It is notoriously high. I've seen 100% in lots of fast-food chains. So, 34% turnover at Starbucks did not seem at all high to me. **But by 2013, my district was recording 19% new-barista turnover within the first 90 days.** With Playbook, new employees were presented with good training and clearly stated tasks, and they became confident in their job skills faster. So, they were not leaving as often. Starbucks' really big draw—healthcare benefits for everyone working at least 20 hours per week, after about 1,000 hours worked—was unchanged. But I think what really makes people happier on the job is that feeling of competence that comes from knowing the work.

Our renewed focus on training and cross-training also resulted in **a rise in the percentage of internal promotions from 50% to 75%.** Using the four-step teaching method popularized by TWI[11]—prepare the learner, demonstrate the work, practice, and follow up—we were constantly teaching partners new skills and preparing them for promotion. This is what we were always supposed to be doing, of course. Playbook just took our good intentions and made training a necessary part of everyone's schedule.

It was a strong story to tell, I thought, as we prepared to introduce Playbook to thousands of stores across the country. And I knew a good story was important. Anyone who has tried to spread a new initiative in a large organization knows it is a tricky proposition. When asking people to work in a new way, resistance

---

11. Training Within Industry (TWI), developed by the US Department of War in 1945 to facilitate training of people new to factory work, remains a reference point for on-the-job training in many companies.

is inevitable. The person leading the effort must be part sales savant, part autocrat—willing to be firm even while cajoling people into trying new and disruptive routines.

My counterpart in Chicago, Steve, and I were asked to step out of our regional director roles and join the lean team in mid-2013 in order to coach others being introduced to Playbook methods. We prepared to roll out to Los Angeles, Dallas, and New York, with a steady rate of transformations moving across the country after that.

What I discovered over the course of the next year is that convincing people to change is really hard, but there's also a tremendous upside to leading the spread of a new operating system. For those of us willing to wade into the work, we get firsthand answers to our most pressing questions.

For instance, let's look back at that question of backsliding. Every new initiative goes through this, I think. No matter how superior the new way seems, people fall back into old patterns. What Steve and I noticed in our own regions, however, was that stores with a high volume of orders seemed to have an easier time sticking to the Playbook.

The busier the store, the easier it was for partners to adopt Playbook methods as their own. It was the same phenomenon we saw during the busiest days in Newtown: the higher the volume got, the more people relied on standardized work routines to deal with the rush.

I knew that partners in rural areas were not less capable than those in downtown Chicago. When I observed people working in lower-volume stores, it was clear to me that they understood the structure of the operating system and the job responsibilities. But it was also clear that roles broke down fast in the slower stores, and it was more difficult for baristas to recover their routines. As we moved into new regions, this pattern held.

After a number of months observing and talking to partners, it became clear that there was a unique burden for partners at low-volume stores. Let's say there are 30 tasks for partners to do on a shift, no matter how many customers they have. Some things, like "make latte," happen repeatedly and are done by one person. Other tasks, such as cleaning and restocking, might happen a handful of times on a shift and get handed back and forth to different people as the plays changed.

When there were 10 people working, partners had somewhere between one and three tasks on their list. When three people were working, they might have two to 15 tasks to remember. Fewer partners on shift meant a longer list of tasks for each person to memorize. And when a new play is called because a partner is added or subtracted from the floor, that means readjusting a half-dozen tasks between the partners.

Simply put, partners in high-volume stores practiced their routines more. Certain plays became familiar, became habits, became second nature.

The fewer the people working, the greater the number of tasks, the more opportunity there was to forget a task and fall out of a carefully synchronized routine. Beyond insisting that our partners in rural areas develop better memories—which, of course, would not be a real solution—how could we support Playbook routines in low-volume environments?

One answer was found in Southington, Connecticut. This was one of those low-volume stores that suffered a lot of backsliding. The partners and leaders were not resistant to the lean operating system. In fact, they were also puzzled as to why they could not hold onto routines, and after some investigation, we found that the problem was one of adjustment.

Think of a volume knob. At high volume, there might be 12 people in specific roles, each accomplishing one or two tasks. After lunch, we turn the volume down by half to match the store traffic. That meant six partners on the floor. If volume fell by half again, we hit our lowest official play. This called for three people on shift: one store support, one barista, and one working the cash register.

In rural Connecticut, however, there were sometimes just two people on shift because business demands called for only two. One person—the shift supervisor—was always in the store-support role. That left the other person to both run the cash register and make drinks. If four or five customers all walked in at the same time, the store-support person would naturally stop filling the pastry case and help out on the register. In that case, who made the brewed coffee when the timer went off? Was the store-support partner supposed to resume replenishment duties immediately? What about the work that had not been finished when he was on the register? Without clear guidance, people made it up as they went along.

Whenever partners fell back into ad hoc work routines, we found, they had a hard time going back to their Playbook routines. And then they had a harder time remembering their tasks and routines.

In Southington, store partners and leaders responded by creating the first official two-person play. They created a new lowest setting on the volume knob by showing how, with just two people on shift, the store-support partner could have a routine that allowed him to help out on the cash register for the space of one coffee cycle. If the store had just two types of brewed coffee on offer, that meant he had about 22 minutes to help customers before returning to his work routine without falling too seriously out of sync. Most times, he might need only 10 minutes to get through a rush, then resume the normal store-support routine.

The Southington store became far more stable when leaders customized the lean operating system to better suit their reality. They were able to do this because they had been trained in the building blocks of the lean system. They understood the machinery behind the plays. This was a critical point that I would take forward. I started talking to people about spreading "best thinking" instead of "best practices." Not everyone agreed.

Do you remember the "Blizzard of Best Practices"? For years, Starbucks had been enamored of them. Someone would come up with a good idea and send it to their regional leader or headquarters in Seattle. If leaders agreed that it was a good idea—whether or not it was a widespread problem—it would be stamped "best practice" and sent out to all the other store managers. Whether this was a good solution for a problem you had or not, you were expected to adopt the practice.

Sure, lots of store managers did not adopt each and every best practice. But even if they didn't, they could be coached about it. Depending on the communication style of their direct supervisor, that coaching could feel pretty negative.

In Southington, I saw how a real understanding of the lean operating system enabled the partners to come up with a better solution than others could have. With training, they were able to apply their best thinking. Everyone in the leadership path, I argued, needed to know how to write a play from scratch.

On the other side of this argument were people who felt the pressure of training tens of thousands of people in a limited amount of time. At this time, we were sticking to the one-month training and preparation for every store transitioning to Playbook. During that month, district managers taught store managers lean concepts and play building; store managers then taught those to their assistant store manager and shift supervisors. Those leaders taught store partners 5S, kanban, and problem solving while cleaning and organizing the store and putting a replenishment system in place. Within months, as employees left and were added, store leaders and partners were training new partners about lean, helping to entrench the knowledge.

It was intensive work, and my colleagues who were focused on our need to go fast came up with their own solution: automation. We should have a computer program that allowed store managers to input some data and have a play presented to them. Then, we would have all the benefits of a lean operating system without having to explain the concepts over and over, they argued.

For me, this solution spelled out a slow death for Playbook. If people in the leadership path were not trained in the fundamental thinking behind a lean operating system, how could they train the next generation of lean thinkers? Without knowledge, how could they customize Playbook to make it work for them? Smaller stores like the one in Southington would have struggled and tried hard and finally dropped any pretense of calling plays because the right play did not exist (until they wrote it).

Without settling this disagreement between going fast and training, we all moved forward. Over the course of a year, I coached the leaders of regions in and around New York City, upstate New York, Newark, Ohio, Pennsylvania, Kentucky, and Washington, DC. I saw the hurdles and setbacks of rolling out Playbook in about 500 stores and noticed another surprisingly common theme—one that is nearly a mirror image to my findings above.

Baristas and cashiers in higher-volume stores adapted to the lean operating system quickly and—much of the time—with real enthusiasm. Limited task lists were easy to remember, and the interlocking routines made work a little easier for everyone. Getting their leaders to adopt the system was sometimes a much harder sell.

It is true that it is easier for people to change tasks than it is to change behavior, which is what is required of leaders. But there was more at play here. The bigger and faster the market, it seemed, the more resistant the leaders.

In dynamic markets, regional and district leaders had a tendency to hold tight to the reins, as if any deviation from the rules could send the whole fast-paced operation careening off the road. One big-city leader, for instance, insisted that the bulletin boards that were in the back room of every store and reserved for company communications should look exactly the same from one store to the next. I was coaching him—let's call him Bob—toward allowing leaders and partners to use the boards to communicate about store-specific improvements and suggestions. But for Bob, a good communications board had the official and updated sales report posted in the lower left corner, followed in precise formation by a printout of the cleanliness report, the marketing report, and whatever other neatly printed computer-generated reports were deemed relevant.

Change can be messy, I told him. How about if we let the morning and afternoon shifts use the board to post their ideas about signals for the replenishment system? Or improvement ideas? But Bob wasn't having it.

I know Bob felt a sense of accomplishment when he toured stores in his region and saw, one after another, those perfectly matching communications boards. While he felt accomplished, however, I'm pretty sure the store partners merely felt compliant. The feeling we were aiming for was engaged.

So, leaders in complex urban markets tended to be reluctant to embrace Playbook, while the store partners were mostly enthusiastic. Meanwhile, leaders in lower-volume areas were more willing to give this new idea a try, even as their store partners struggled. Why?

Smaller markets were constantly overshadowed by their big-city counterparts. This is probably true in any company. High-volume stores posted impressive receipts; they were watched closely by internal and external analysts; they were destinations for corporate visits and had big design budgets. I do not think Howard Shultz ever went to Southington. So, when someone like me comes in and invites these leaders to learn new ideas and discover the cutting edge of retail, they were very interested. Baristas and cashiers in the low-volume stores may have been struggling with the new routines, but their managers were among our best cheerleaders.

It was an interesting pattern. I began every coaching session by asking leaders about their biggest problems. Then, we talked about how the lean operating system could be put to work addressing those problems. I heard a diversity of problems but became accustomed to hearing similar themes. Leaders from complex, dynamic markets had trouble staying fully staffed and did not really believe that frontline partners could help solve problems. In many cases, they feared giving over problem-solving and decision-making control to others. With these people, I talked a lot about the benefits of an engaged frontline workforce and, in the end, pointed out that the leader probably did not have enough hours in the day to fix every issue that arose. So, maybe it was a good thing to teach others how to find solutions.

In the lower-volume markets, we talked a lot about labor-to-transactions ratios and how to make it work. In a small town, our stores that were open in the evening were often slow. Let's say there were 30 transactions in an hour. In the current best thinking, one transaction every two minutes was a slow, easy cadence for one person to handle. But the truth was that customers arrived in bunches. Stores either were empty or had a line of people six deep at the register.

In these markets, the most pertinent business question leaders had was often, "How do I increase traffic in the evening enough to justify a third person on shift?"

Again, I would counsel against jumping to solutions. Maybe trying to get more customers in the door would solve things. But maybe the market would not support this. Instead of starting with the answer, I asked these leaders to present the question to store partners: "How do we serve customers who do not flow in an even cadence?"

Asking the right question is how the partners in Southington came up with their two-person play. The play worked so well that this little off-the-highway store lost its reputation for slow evening service. As efficiency increased, so did demand. Finally, sales figures justified the addition of a third person on shift, and they returned to the standard playbook.

I collected stories like these—of good training triumphing over sticky problems—as I kept arguing for a robust training system. Every leader, from stores large and small, needed to know not just how to call a play but also how to write one. They needed to know how to pull the system apart and examine the gears.

I argued, but I also found evidence of homemade work-arounds. In one store, I found laminated cards with prewritten plays. This might have been all right, but they were written for another store, using that store's data. The manager there had generously provided her prewritten plays for colleagues who did not have the time or understanding to write their own. All we needed to do was ask the manager how her expected product mix in this half hour was determining how partners were assigned to roles to see that she did not understand what she was doing. The business acumen I promised them was getting lost.

Then I came across two more stores with the same laminated cards and tried to send an alarm up the chain. What I heard in return was that these cards were important safety nets for busy store managers. They were offered as supports. I strongly felt they were impediments to the future of the system but understood that not every manager was going to embrace the ideas and results of Playbook as zealously as me.

* * *

Less than a year after I began this broader introduction of Playbook, I was asked to take on a new role. As director of operations for the license stores of New York and New England, I was responsible for about 200 Starbucks locations that were licensed to other companies. These included stand-up cafés in grocery stores, train stations, and hotels and more traditional looking cafés in universities and airports.

Most of these locations were managed by a larger business. The food-service management arm of the airport authority, for instance, usually employs and supervises baristas in an airport Starbucks. If low employee turnout is a problem at the Cinnabon, that management company might shuffle a barista over there—after a change of apron, of course.

I knew that it would be difficult to introduce Playbook in this environment, but I was determined. I was excited to introduce lean thinking to these management companies. I was offering them a free course in a proven method for improving their businesses.

This is what I told my eight district managers—all employed by Starbucks—who would be the front line in convincing these management companies to adopt our methods in the cafés under their roofs. We were offering licensees a gift.

Store managers, who worked for the dozen or so management companies I interacted with, were often receptive to the ideas and to the attention from their district managers. But their paychecks came from the management company.

Some of those management companies were mildly interested in hearing about how a big successful company like Starbucks was managing its operations. But really, they had to see tangible results for their own businesses in order to invest. But they could not get results without an up-front investment of time and attention. Getting most of those companies to learn and teach Playbook was a lot like pushing a rope.

The Starbucks at Logan Airport in Boston, for instance, was one of our busiest stores. I knew that a lean operating system would really help baristas work through some of the airport's epic rush periods, if only we could stabilize store staffing. This was one of the management companies that liked to move employees around a lot, and we never knew how many people would be working on a given day or time slot.

So, when it was time for our district manager to kick off Playbook in that store with an all-hands meeting, I went and invited representatives of the management company to join us. When I arrived at the agreed-upon time, however, less than half of the store's staff was available for the kickoff and first training session. I was accommodating and cheerful as we made plans to try again on a day when the management company could really get everyone there.

The next big day arrived, and there were even fewer staff members available to be trained. I remember that it was just three people. The airport's manager of food service was also there, at my invitation. He looked around a little bemused and said, "It looks like you have a problem here."

Now, I am a very positive person and unfailingly polite. I work hard at it sometimes and am proud of having a generally good attitude. It surprised me as well as him when I did not smile in return. I looked him dead in the eye and said, "Clearly, you do have a problem." I turned and left.

Our next scheduled kickoff and training took place with about 20 people, and, as I predicted, certain elements of the system were quickly embraced. In a very busy store with periodic spikes in traffic, Playbook was a great ally. Managers learned to staff for customer demand. Teaching new employees the job was easier when the curriculum was the standardized work of the various plays.

And in some cases, we were able to make the wider impact I had envisioned. In a Target store in upstate New York, for instance, I had baristas who were learning about lean from a very engaged district manager. After discovering 5S, they attacked the small storeroom set aside for Starbucks within the larger Target storeroom. People working in the Target storeroom took notice and soon started stealing some of the ideas they saw. Our district manager threw in a little coaching to the Target employees who were interested, and, next we heard, those organizational practices were being spread to Target stores all over the region.

Knowing that we could have a positive impact was heartening, but, overall, we were still pushing rope. The fact is I'm still not sure whether a lean operating system can take root and grow in an organization whose leadership does not actively seek that transformation and support it. I had some ideas about how a transplant or a grafted limb on a tree could effect change in the host or larger organization, but I never really saw it occur.

This did not dim my enthusiasm for a lean operating system. It just underlined the necessity of it being championed by leadership. At Starbucks, the system was created and disseminated by a lean team working out of Seattle, with the blessing of at least one member of the C-suite. Before we were even finished rolling it out, however, that lean team at headquarters was dissolving. Scott left. Then Josh, Hollie, and Brent pursued their own new opportunities. While the Playbook system was still operating and had tremendous regional champions, there was no chief executive cheerleader.

* * *

During that 2008 conference in New Orleans, Cliff Burrows, president of our US business, said that we were going to learn more about the work of our baristas in order to make it better for them. We had done that. Burrows also promised Howard Shultz that we would save $25 million through waste reduction. I believe we did that, too.[12]

What we lacked was leadership resolve to remain a lean operation, to train all incoming employees in the basics, and to push ourselves further in understanding and implementing lean thinking. As one concession or adjustment after another was made, the level of lean capability began to slide.

After I left Starbucks in 2015 to work for the Lean Enterprise Institute, I found myself in a Starbucks four or five times a week for a tall triple-shot Americano. It's still my favorite coffee. And I can't help but watch the play being performed behind the counter. I spot the shift supervisor easily enough by the timer clipped to their apron, indicating when the next brew cycle begins. I watch the paths

12. In my region, we reduced coffee waste by about half, and the same for dairy. This was measured by inventory variance, in which we compared what we had in stock to what we should have had, based on actual usage plus a 20% buffer. The coffee bean variance went from 2.1 pounds per store per day to less than one. Gallons of dairy product went from 4.1 per store per day to 2.0.

people take as they perform their duties. If the timer goes off and the shift supervisor—always in the store-support role—immediately goes to brew more coffee, I am cheered. I take it as a good omen into my day.

While I am working with a diversity of businesses these days, helping them to better understand lean thinking and train their employees, I find myself thinking of Starbucks often and what I learned there. It is amazing to me how applicable those lessons are for others.

Nine Lessons to Share

1. Go see

2. Standardization can set us free

3. Freedom requires careful preparation

4. Best thinking is preferable to best practices

5. Respect beginners

6. Beware of the next Big Thing

7. Respect for people means taking care with your questions

8. A truly excellent people-development program does not spring from training alone

9. Make a strategic partner out of HR

Nine Lessons to Share

One

If there was just one lesson from Starbucks that I could impart to business leaders it would be this: **Go see.** Go watch people and machines as they interact to create value for the customer and, in doing so, to provide your paycheck. Learn how the work gets done and then go watch it again to see whether it is still done that way the next day. Be curious about what you see.

Make it part of your regular routine to go see. If you feel like an unnecessary limb out there, lost amid the value-producing work being done at the front lines, create a list of respectful questions to ask. Get to know people doing the work and ask about ideas they have for improving their work.

There are a lot of people who want to lock you in your office or cubicle and keep you hunched all day in front of the glowing screen of your email queue or spreadsheets. If you defy them and walk out to where the work is being done and truly see it on a regular basis, this will become the best part of your day.

I know this because in my family, we do a lot of fly-fishing. That might seem like a non sequitur but trust me on this. Every spring here in Connecticut, when the ice is still patchy on the ground and green shoots are just beginning to show, we start dreaming of days spent in hip waders, feeling the steady pull of the Farmington River against our legs as we cast fishing lines in long arcs over our heads. The Farmington has the best trout fishing east of the Mississippi River, and we have come to know sections of that river like we know our backyard.

Fishing is full of rituals. The first ritual in spring is data collection. Of course, we don't call it that. But in spring, my husband and I cannot stop ourselves from driving slowly along the river, looking for new pools created by animals, downed trees, and fast currents. We stop and talk to others who are out there doing the same thing. We talk about snow melt and look for signs of the first hatch of the Hendrickson mayfly (*Ephemerella subvaria*). Trout gorge themselves on those mayflies; when they hatch, we know the fish will be in an eating frenzy.

When our oldest son, Louis, was younger, he and Brian would spend hours on that river, getting to know each other better as they drove and walked and talked about what they saw. When it came time to fish, they hardly had to discuss what they were doing as they stood in the river, poles like metronomes, Brian's hand-tied flies flashing in the sun overhead.

What we have learned about going to see is that it enriches our experience. Catching first sight of the March brown fly (*Vicarium fuscum*) in mid-June or recognizing the tiny blue-winged olives (*Baetis*) when they come out in fall, is actually thrilling. These are not annoying insects. These are signals of change, indicating that we need to switch out our flies and that another season is opening up.

If we were to wade out into the Farmington in April not knowing what was up around the bend, our fishing would be almost certainly fruitless. It would not be fun. Catching fish is the point, after all, even if we do set them free again. As former rock climbers who managed to escape injury, Brian and I are perhaps on the serious side of preparedness. But if you think about any hobby or sport—or business, for that matter—preparation and planning are half the fun and certainly the key to attaining good results.

This is the mind-set we need to take with us to work. We should anticipate going to see operations on a regular basis, knowing it will enrich our understanding of reality. The monthly or annual executive tour will no longer be enough. Then we need to teach *go-see* to our direct reports—both the attitude and the practice. Most of us will need to coax our bosses into seeing the work, as well.

When Scott, Josh, and Hollie were putting together the Playbook system, they began by spending weeks in stores in Portland, Oregon, and Northern California, experimenting in real situations. When they set up the demonstration laboratory in Seattle, they invited in senior executives to introduce the lean operating system, knowing that there is no substitute for seeing the work in real time.

Because the original lean team used the go-see principle, Playbook worked. Because we made go-see an ongoing piece of the management system, Playbook continued to work.

Two

Here is the most surprising lesson I learned from Starbucks: **Standardization can set us free**. It sounds like a slogan from George Orwell, I know. And, having worked in the fast-food industry for most of three decades, I know that standardized work on the front line is a tough sell. Nobody wants to be treated like a robot.

Yet, I saw it happen during the worst week of our lives in Newtown, and then saw it happen again in all kinds of stores when the pace of work quickened: when baristas embraced the standardization of necessary tasks, they had more time for human interaction. When we get to the point that we do not have to think about the next motion required to get the job done, we have more space in our lives.

Psychologists have a term for what we are doing: "decision fatigue avoidance." People like Steve Jobs and Mark Zuckerberg were known for wearing the same style of clothing every day in order to avoid what-to-wear decisions, freeing their minds for more meaningful decisions.

Every bit of work we do requires a dozen decisions. Approach the machine from the left or the right? Hold the tool flat or upright? Is the milk warm enough? If we help people find a set of repeatable actions to accomplish the job, we help them avoid decision fatigue. If they are not fatigued, they can put energy into relationships and make better decisions outside of their standardized work.

In a manufacturing environment, I have seen people use that extra space to check their tools and the quality of incoming material. In healthcare and service industries, we can use it to chat a little, to ask questions, and to listen to others—to be more human.

What's important is how we frame the concept of standardized work as it is introduced. It is the highest form of respect to engage people in thinking through how work is accomplished. But too many times, I have seen leaders skip right past the introduction, as if they could just tell people what to do and have it be so. If people do not have a compelling reason to do it your way, they will quickly return to doing it how they please.

Be prepared to introduce standardized work with a few points on how it will benefit people in their work. People need to be given the opportunity to see and understand problems and then apply tools to resolve issues they face. Then be prepared to show how using the prescribed set of actions will interface with the work of coworkers. Have a clearly stated improvement process to allow people to make changes to the standardized work that will benefit everyone.

Three

Standardized work can set you free, but **freedom requires careful preparation**. Creating an environment where standardized work can flourish means studying the work as it is accomplished by the front line, solving problems, and training people in both the actions and the reasons why.

In too many places, standardized work is written by engineers, far from the front line. Even at Starbucks, we sometimes gave in to this temptation. We emphasized problem solving at the front line, but those Better Ways—detailing exactly how to brew coffee, load the pastry case, make an espresso—were written in Seattle.

There will always be a bias among top managers to create more centralized control, especially in a large organization. Who really knows how to do the work? Is it the people on the front line or the people with a broader scope and bigger title? Since one of our objectives was to create a similar customer experience across all stores, maybe we did need to have this dual approach where frontline problem solving bubbled up to create a single standardized work solution.

The goal for lean practitioners, however, should always be designing standardized work as close to the customer as possible. In large multisite companies, this can cause an on-going debate between centralized and decentralized control. I find that the clearest answer is to draw a line between standards and methods. Companies set standards, such as saying that every guest must be greeted. But stating exactly how a guest should be greeted—the method—should be left to the people doing the work.

So, centralized leaders set standards and tell individual site leaders that they must have a clearly stated method for achieving that standard, while customer-facing employees and their managers create the standardized work (the method). This maintains control while ensuring that frontline employees—tomorrow's leaders—are trained in creating and maintaining standardized work and solving problems.

In my experience, Starbucks districts and stores that relied solely on the Better Ways, dropping the emphasis on local problem solving, undercut their ability to maintain standardized work. No matter how perfectly conceived, standardized work will always bring problems to the surface, and frontline managers and partners need to be trained in both the theories and the practice of lean thinking in order to solve those problems. When people on the front line know how to observe the work and how to apply scientific thinking to solve problems, and when they understand the benefits of standardized work, it will truly be theirs.

Four

Best thinking is preferable to best practices. When spreading the initial work of lean thinking, everyone is tempted to tell the new sites what worked best in the old sites. Someone will say, "Why reinvent the wheel every time?"

The best response to this is, "Don't jump to solutions."

Best practices are, simply, someone else's solutions. Those best practices solved problems at the original site. The questions we should be asking are, "Do we have the same problem in this new site? Will this best-practice solution give the same result? What will people at the new site lose by not solving their own problems?"

Certainly, best practices can be offered to teams at the store level as background information for their own problem solving. But if a frontline team is going to own the process, they need to decide whether that solution works for that store.

Five

This leads us to the next lesson: **Respect beginners**. Every new site was learning this operating system for the first time. When we introduced the concept of Playbook at the first seed stores, I told those baristas and managers that we were embarking on a completely new era, that we had the opportunity to revolutionize the retail industry. The ideas we were implementing would put us on the forward wave of retail operations, I said. I absolutely meant it, and they knew it.

The people who work in an alpha site—the model cell—often become ardent supporters of lean operating systems. Their work is carefully observed. They are asked for input and listened to. Their problems get solved, and they help to create standardized work. They work closely with leadership to find answers.

Two years later, for the eighty-ninth store kicking off Playbook, I did not have the same energy. I was in danger of presenting a done deal. This is when leaders begin to develop and use jargon, to abbreviate explanations. They say things like, "We have been doing this for 18 months now, and we can tell you blah blah blah." If you are already looking over the heads of the people you are talking to, thinking about the next new store, it is disrespectful.

Keeping it fresh can seem like a tall order when you have 500 sites. Leaders quite naturally become desensitized to the feelings of absolute beginners unless they consciously guard against this.

I learned to create a leadership routine to consciously keep my enthusiasm fresh. Everyone needed to know, each time, that we were on the leading edge of big, new ideas. After all, these partners were the future of this system that I believed in. And new people bring fresh eyes to problems if we encourage them. We need these beginners just like they need our undivided attention.

Six

While respecting the beginners, we also need to **beware of the next Big Thing**. When we were creating and implementing the lean operating system, it was exciting to announce results to my boss, to show off stores running smoothly with better productivity and partner satisfaction. It was like a revolution.

A few years later, I was presenting incremental improvements and talking about solutions we found for small, intractable problems. This required that I learn how to talk about how small demonstrated behaviors would collectively affect key performance indicators. I became more practiced in recognizing predictors of success or failure. Still, it was nowhere near as sexy as showing a brand new system.

We are all addicted to the new. Social media has us constantly clamoring for the next thing. Any parent knows how challenging it is to turn off the smartphones and video games and coax everyone outside to find fun in games their grandparents might have played.

And yet, this is exactly what this kind of work demands—people who can work within it to observe, uncover problems, and stabilize operations. So, what do we do when someone waves a bright, shiny new flag and points in a different direction?

The first question to ask is, "What is being proposed, a program or an operating system?" There is a vast difference between the two. A word processing program, for instance, works only when it is compatible with and driven by a computer's overall operating system. Programs are discrete functions, meant to address a certain kind of need. An operating system is the business's architecture.

Most new ideas are programs. Even Toyota has introduced new programs over the years. The successful programs worked with the operating system. Those that could not be integrated with lean thinking were not successful.

Lean thinking is the first true operating system I can think of since the introduction of management by objectives (MBO) in the first half of the past century. A program in the MBO system would have required a set of measurable goals or objectives to drive the behavior of managers. A program in a lean thinking system, on the other hand, requires that it drive behaviors desirable for this system: respect for people, continuous improvement through structured problem solving, and focus on value for the customer.

New programs can be exciting and beneficial. They just cannot be allowed to throw the entire operating system off course.

Seven

Respect for people means taking care with your questions. Sometimes we ask questions to get answers. Take care not to load your queries with predetermined solutions. This is an easy habit to fall into. I have actually heard district managers squeeze their opinions into thinly veiled questions like this: "It looks like you don't have enough people working. How are you going to call someone in to help cover?"

A more respectful sentence might be, "How many people does the Playbook plan call for? And how many are working?"

But this question, too, has an attitude too aggressive for many people. The answer will probably tell you whether the store manager really understands how to build a staffing plan to meet demand. But it does not build trust.

Sometimes, the best query is not a question but an invitation, such as: "Because I see customers waiting, it makes me believe there are not enough people working. Stand with me and watch the work for a moment. Let's talk about how to create a better experience."

Eight

A truly excellent people-development program does not spring from training alone. I worked with all of the biggest QSRs in the United States, and I know the money and effort they sank into their "Hamburger Universities." There was training for entry-level employees, new leaders, and middle managers inside formal class-rooms with professional teachers. And then all of those students went back to the reality of their home restaurants and had to balance theory with reality in any way they could. A lot gets lost in this type of translation.

For instance, let's say you are an assistant store manager learning to be a manager. One important component of your education is learning how to create an effective schedule. So, you go to Hamburger University—all the big chains have something like this—and learn about peaks and average demand and how to use the software that will help you create the schedule that will deeply affect all of your coworkers' lives. The idea is that you will return to the restaurant and practice this new skill under your manager's tutelage. But the shift is two people short, and your manager cannot come off of the floor to help you. You might be able to ask the manager a couple of questions, but there is rarely time for more than that. You do the best that you can.

The manager glances over the schedule that you printed out, and it looks acceptable. It is posted on the wall. And then all hell breaks loose because the overburdened manager did not tell you about the special scheduling requests that people had submitted, and your schedule seems to be ignoring people's needs. Your first foray into management is not going well.

A really good people-development course requires on-going training and coaching. I found that Starbucks' Playbook system supported on-going training in two important ways. First, giving shift supervisors the job of calling the plays meant that they needed to know how to write a play. Writing a play required knowledge of work components—e.g., how much time tasks took, who was trained to do that work, customer demand of that component—as well as schedules and use of POS data. Since we were often in need of new shift supervisors, we learned that we needed to be constantly training these skills.

Our second support structure was, in some ways, even more important: using the management system's interlocking series of status meetings to consistently check in with everyone's succession planning and skills development. While we had off-site training programs like a Hamburger University, we also had on-going coaching and training in the stores. And we checked on the progress of that coaching through our management status meetings. Because of the constant attention, with store managers needing to report on the skills development of all their people every month, we could emphasize on-going training like off-site programs never could.

If you think about that Black Friday in the Holyoke Mall, where a shift supervisor was prepared and eager to take over all the duties associated with leading the store on the busiest day of the year, you will have a sense as to why I believe Starbucks' training was so effective. Because he had been calling plays for months, that shift supervisor understood more about effectively running a business than store managers in a lot of fast-food restaurants.

Playbook required that we consistently train store partners in various aspects of running the business, ensuring that we had a steady supply of people who could write and call plays. Ultimately, it was the best talent development and succession program I have experienced.

Nine

Make a strategic partner out of HR. At the beginning of your lean transformation, invite the expertise and assistance of HR leaders. Finance really needs to be in on the ground floor, too. In fact, if I could imagine a best-case scenario for a lean launch, it would be with leaders of operations, HR, and finance working as a triumvirate, leveraging one another's subject matter expertise to make business decisions.

Think of all the ways that HR can influence or control the work in operations. In most organizations, HR is responsible for setting hiring standards. They can emphasize hiring people who see themselves as problem solvers or as lone-wolf entrepreneurial types. They can emphasize work experience or leadership skills. HR leaders are involved in writing the criteria for performance reviews, setting pay scales, and usually have oversight in employee skills training. In other words, HR is deeply influential over the makeup of the workforce and the common drivers of employee behavior.

Meanwhile, finance drives the managers. People in the finance department are usually responsible for writing and updating policies such as revenue-to-labor ratios. They end up telling store managers how many people they should have on staff and on shift in order to make their balance sheets work.

For instance, at Starbucks the finance rule used to be that store managers should have one person on staff for every $1,000 in average store revenue. If you were a $30,000-a-week store, you had 30 full-time equivalents on staff. As far as these kinds of rules go, it was perfectly clear. But it left no room to actually change or improve the financial dynamics of a store.

Then Playbook was introduced and we told managers to staff based on customer demand. Once we separated staffing from revenue, we set ourselves on a collision course with the folks in finance. And this is the kind of friction between departments that can completely derail a lean initiative.

It turned out that staffing to customer demand did not produce a hugely different answer from staffing based on revenue. We usually found that we needed more or less partners on different shifts than there had been, but the overall staffing was not changed. Still, the managers were stressed. They did not like hearing that they needed to do one thing coming from corporate finance in Seattle and then another from the very earnest and enthusiastic regional director at the door.

Similar early tensions played out with HR. I am not certain whether anyone even told the leaders in HR that we were beginning the Playbook rollout. I know we did not really involve them for the initial training sessions in the field. And trouble showed up early.

Remember the Westport store in Connecticut that had a strong-willed store manager and very busy rush hours? The initial weeks were rocky, and turnover among baristas spiked. I discussed the problem with our regional HR leader, Joyce, during our regular monthly meeting. We talked about the new behaviors needed from store managers, and then Joyce, who was based in New Jersey, said the three words that were music to my ears, "Let's go see."

So, she and I went to Westport and watched Suzie muscle through a rush with rapid-fire orders to her crew. Then we went to West Hartford and watched Courtney model the behavior we wanted. She asked respectful questions and coached partners to stay on track in their roles. When we asked Courtney to tell us how they solved a particular problem, she invited the shift supervisor over to explain the problem-solving process. Courtney did not have a turnover problem.

Joyce not only understood what we were aiming for but also went back and explained to her HR colleagues what we were doing. HR rewrote the core competencies required of managers and supervisors in a Playbook environment and even produced a reference book showing what effective problem solving looked like at every level of leadership. In writing that book and the new core competencies, HR took a lot of the guesswork out of identifying who was management material. They made the leader-selection process more transparent and therefore more respectful.

HR, finance, and other functional departments can present enormous roadblocks to a lean transformation, or they can assist in ways we cannot even imagine.

***

Much of this work is about laying a good foundation and then being open to seeing—really seeing—how everything interacts. There is a moment like this that happens on the Farmington River. When Brian and my sons and I have done the early work of going to see the river's conditions, when the insects have hatched and the flies have been tied and we are finally fishing, there is a moment when it is just me and the water pushing against my hip waders and my fishing line shushing overhead as it arcs back and forth that I disappear into everything, into the landscape all around.

Or watching my son Louis swirl his entire line overhead and drop his fly gently into the waiting mouth of a rainbow trout, or when Brian steps into deep water and fights with the current as the fish on the end of his line leaps out of the water. We always look to each other in these moments because the shared victory is sweeter.

It is magical, but it only comes from doing the work: going to see, preparing the foundation, and—in the case of working with a lean operating system—being willing to change the way you interact with people.

The moment that we become curious instead of controlling, I am sure, is a moment that we take a step toward becoming better leaders. When we find real joy in seeing the eyes of a team member light up with sudden comprehension, we become the kind of leader who makes a meaningful, lasting impression.

A lean operating system is never just confined to operations. It affects every facet of an organization and all the people in it, whether the company has one site or 10,000. A transformation like this will take any organization through triumphs and struggles, and people will be changed as a result.

After all, a lean operating system is not a static thing. It is not a latte, I used to say. It's a growing ecosystem that needs nurturing and attention. When you think the work is done, that means you have probably stopped paying attention.

I am still surprised at the twists and turns our story took. We had several iterations of going to see the work and then learning and relearning how to solve problems before we began to see real change. And then when change happened, it was like a wave that gathered its own energy.

Because of that change, we were able to find peace and inspiration while working within the eye of a terrible tragedy.

The great American poet and essayist Henry David Thoreau said, "It's not what you look at that matters, it's what you see." After my experiences, I would expand upon that. To do this work, we need to be able to truly see, and then we must allow ourselves—our minds, our actions—to be changed. To see the truth and be changed by it is how we evolve.

About the Author

Karen has over 30 years' experience leading, training, and coaching high-performance teams of staff and executives in rapid-growth environments. She built a consistent track record of growing the number of retail stores along with the continuous improvement capabilities of people.

At Starbucks, Karen made recommendations on the creation of an operating system model line, then led the first application in a working store and provided feedback necessary for a broad, global implementation. She also led a team of coaches responsible for teaching problem solving and mentoring skills to regional executives, directors, and district managers responsible for implementing the lean operating system. Karen led the growth of Starbucks' New England market.

Previously, Karen held management and executive posts in operations, marketing, and training at large restaurant chains, a retail consulting company, and a technology startup preparing for an initial public offering.

As part of the management team at LEI, Karen leads the educational experiences Lean Enterprise Institute provides out to the public.

Acknowledgments

I am grateful for the leadership lessons both technical and social, provided throughout the lean transformation designed by Scott Heydon, Josh Howell, Hollie Jensen, and Brent Moden. I hold myself accountable to sharing these lessons with other business leaders in meaningful ways. As the lean team in a global organization such as Starbucks, Scott, Josh, Hollie, Lara and Brent were pioneers and set a high bar. Each of them inspired me and many others to see a better way. Their work will continue to transform the retail industry and improve the lives of the people who do the work. Thank you for your coaching, guidance, encouragement and, above all, for expecting me to build the required technical capability and personal understanding to better serve my team, my customers and ultimately the business in which I led.

Thank you to Bethany Thompson (Gness), David Carini, Alan McNeil, Emily Filc, Alison Perreault, Alida Kronsberg, Courtney Cheever, Frank DiAmico, Peter Torrbierte, and Jen Cho for your leadership courage and ability to learn a new way of thinking. Your capability, dedication, perseverance and demonstrated success through transformation changed the trajectory of our team, our business and the company. Our time together represented one of the most rewarding experiences of my career. The impact of your work is measurable far beyond what is seen on the surface.

Additionally, to the district manager team above, thank you to Vivian Hunnicutt, Steve Devizio, Joyce Varino (RIP), Zeta Smith, Mike Dowling, Hester Chang, David Bailey, Leslie Fratto, Theresa Papcunik, Cathy Iannaccone, Jessica Boelts, Diane Platt, Jean Ortega, Kelly McEllroy, Peter Quattro and Lori Turci for answering the call. What an honor it was for me to be on your team when the community needed us most.

Thanks Jeff Smith for his encouragement and help as I to continue to build my technical understanding and translate my learning. The development approach you practice, through revealing fine layers of knowledge inside of increments of repetitive learning, is the foundation on which we all developed.

Closing the wide gap of thinking between the executives who develop the business strategies for success and the people who do the work to deliver on those strategies is a long a winding road. The way that the work is designed, the problems that become exposed, and the management system that facilitates the solutions has shown to be a path worth taking. Having the courage to take the path and stay the course over time is not taken lightly. Thanks to Mark Reich for pushing me past my fears while in the process of writing this book. I did not make it obvious or known at the time.

Thank you John Shook for sharing your wisdom and expertise. I have heard you refer to yourself as an anthropologist, the definition of which is:

Noun:

1. A person that studies the origins, physical and cultural development, biological characteristics, and social custom and beliefs of humankind.
2. A student of humans and their works.

To share in this experience with you has been profound and metamorphic.

Thanks to Jim Womack for his dedication to changing the world through helping me and so many other business leaders understand lean thinking. Your input and guidance throughout the development process of this book has been essential. Your kindness and endearing partnership has been a precious gift.

It is with the deepest respect and gratitude I thank Emily Adams for her partnership in bringing this story to life. My Friday night conversations with her will forever be a cherished memory of a bridge in time that she so gracefully helped me walk across.

I continue to become aware of how much more there is to learn and understand.

Karen

Index

Made in the USA
Las Vegas, NV
01 February 2023

66688070R00069